C I T Y P A C K
Munich

By Te

Fodor's

Fodor's Travel Publications
New York • Toronto • London • Sydney • Auckland

WWW.FODORS.COM

Contents

About this book

Citypack Munich is divided into six sections to cover the six most important aspects of your visit to Munich. It includes:

- The city and its people
- Itineraries, walks, and excursions
- The top 25 sights to visit
- What makes the city special
- Restaurants, hotels, stores, and nightlife
- Practical information

In addition, easy to read side panels provide fascinating extra facts and snippets, highlights of places to visit, and invaluable practical advice.

CROSS-REFERENCES

To help you make the most of your visit, cross-references, indicated by ▶ , show you where to find additional information about a place or subject.

MAPS

The fold-out map in the wallet at the back of the book is a comprehensive street plan of Munich. All the map references given in the book refer to this map. For example, the BMW-Museum on Petuelring 130 has the following information: ➕ J22—indicating the grid square of the map in which the BMW-Museum will be found.

The city-center maps found on the inside front and back covers of the book itself are for quick reference. They show the Top 25 Sights, described on pages 24–48, which are clearly plotted by number (❶–㉕, not page number) from west to east.

ADMISSION CHARGES

An indication of the admission charge (for all attractions) is given by categorizing the standard adult rate as follows:
✋ expensive (over DM10; over 5 euros), moderate (DM5–10; 2.5–5 euros), and inexpensive (under DM5; under 2.5 euros).

MUNICH *life*

INTRODUCING MUNICH

Surveys show that given the choice, over half the German population would choose to live in Munich, Bavaria's capital. It is more than just an attractive city. It radiates a unique atmosphere that is hard to define although many have tried: "village of a million," "metropolis with a heart," "Athens on the Isar," "the secret capital of Germany."

The Glockenspiel, New Town Hall

To understand Munich, you really need to understand the Bavarian people. It is their strong sense of patriotism and deep-rooted conservatism that underpins the city, creating a rare balance of German urban efficiency and rural Alpine romanticism. The best time to visit is spring or summer; long hazy months when even the blue skies with their fleecy white clouds mirror the Free State's national colors. Look closely and you will see that blue and white diamonds dominate every aspect of Munich life, from the BMW logo to the livery of its famous breweries.

Green Munich

Munich is ideally located less than an hour from the Alps and a stone's throw from Austria, Italy, and Switzerland, so on the weekends, there is always a mass exodus to nearby villages, lakes, and mountains whatever the season. Summer, however, belongs to Munich's English Garden. And the River Isar, with activities ranging from beach barbecues to nude sunbathing, is more alive than any other city river in the world.

The clichéd image many have of a "typical" German is actually a Bavarian, sporting leather shorts, feasting on sausage and dumplings, and accompanied by a *Dirndl*-clad lady armed with at least a dozen huge mugs of beer (27 is the current record). For here, *Lederhosen* and felt hats with tufts resembling shaving brushes are *de rigueur*, part of a cherished centuries-old folk tradition, and an outward proclamation of Bavarian proud individuality. Don't worry if you can't understand the dialect—most Germans have the same problem.

Native-born Münchners are a rarity. The majority of inhabitants come from other parts of Germany, although they all regard themselves as citizens of Munich in spirit. Nearly a quarter of the population is foreign, so

Munich has a truly international flavor. The city's social scene is fast and fun. A thriving student population crams into the bars and cafés of trendy Schwabing, but Munich is also a city of writers, artists, musicians, and movie-makers, the rich and the jet-set, who cruise the boulevards in their Porsche convertibles. It is in the old town center around Marienplatz where the city's heart beats loudest.

Take the U-Bahn (subway) at 6AM and you will find a lot of sleepy-looking people going to work. These are your average Münchners: diligent, efficient, dedicated to their work but even more dedicated to their *Freizeit* (free time). Perhaps it is the proximity to Italy that causes lunch hours to get longer and the working day to get shorter? Come 3PM, many are back on the U-Bahn, and heading for the city's legendary beer gardens,—Münchners' real joy is to drink a cool beer in the shade of chestnut trees in the English Garden. The jovial atmosphere of the beer gardens, where social distinctions cease to matter, brings out the best in everyone: the Bavarian *joie de vivre*, a passion for outdoor life, sociability, and determination to

A mystery wind

Munich's continental climate guarantees icy winters and hot summers, but there is also the famous föhn, a wind that can blow up at any time of year. This warm, dry, Alpine wind guarantees amazing crystal-clear views (the Alps seem almost close enough to touch), on the one hand; on the other it is blamed for headaches and bad moods. So if drivers seem more wreckless, barmaids more short-tempered and locals blunter than usual, you may hear it blamed on the föhn!

Enjoying a beer in the English Garden

Munich life

"How can one speak of Munich but to say it is a kind of German heaven? Some people sleep and dream they are in paradise, but all over Germany people sometimes dream they have gone to Munich." Thomas Wolfe, 1925

"Don't bother going anywhere else ... nothing can match Munich. Everything else in Germany is a waste of time." Ernest Hemingway, 1923

Musician from an oom-pah band

enjoy. If it's not the beer garden, its the beer keller that everyone crowds to after work or on weekends. Here, as in the beer gardens, you'll find people from all walks of life joining together on tressle tables for a chat over a foaming *Maß* (stein) of beer. Don't be surprised if a stranger suddenly links arms with you to sway to the music of an oom-pah band.

Beer plays an unashamedly important role in Munich life. Where else in the world is drinking considered the main activity for weeks at a stretch, and its beer festivals counted as "seasons"? Munich's breweries also play a key role in the town's economy, alongside a thriving service industry. After Frankfurt, Munich is Germany's largest banking center, headquarters of the country's insurance sector, a top center of fashion and movie-making, the world's second publishing and media city after New York, and Germany's second-largest industrial city. It has a reputation as Germany's most expensive city; spiraling rents and expensive public transportation put the cost of living beyond the reach of many people.

The Bavarian capital's close associations with the rise of Nazism can't be overlooked. However, after World War II, although half its buildings were reduced to rubble, the city moved on. Unlike so many German cities it chose to restore and reconstruct the great palaces and churches of its more distant past, in the process re-creating one of Europe's most beautiful cities, one full of historic buildings, handsome parks and fine museums, galleries, and theaters.

So what *is* Munich all about? A village of a million or a bustling metropolis? A mixture of central European efficiency and Mediterranean atmosphere, of BMW and the bohemian, of technology and tradition, or just a *gemütlich*, good-time city? Come and find out for yourself.

MUNICH IN FIGURES

A welcoming sign

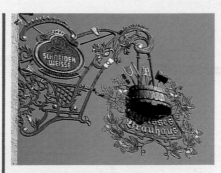

People
- Population in 2000: 1,315,254, including 269,653 foreigners.
- Historical growth: 100,000 in 1846; 829,000 in 1939; 480,000 in 1945; 1,000,000 in 1957.
- Religion: 56 percent Roman Catholic, 20 percent Protestant.
- Number of students at Munich University (Germany's largest): 102,000.
- Number of visitors annually: 50 million day visitors, over 7 million overnight stays.

Leisure
- Entertainment: 84 movie theaters, 53 bookstores, 46 museums, 48 theaters, 3 orchestras.
- Number of sports clubs: 655.
- Area of parkland: 10,331 acres.
- Number of bicycle owners: 25,000.
- Bicycle paths: 808 miles.

Geography
- Area of city: 120 square miles.
- Number of districts: 41.
- Annual temperature range: -13°F to 92°F.
- Annual hours of sunshine: 1,797.
- Distance from Alps: 30 miles.

Beer
- Number of breweries: 7.
- Annual production: 88 million gallons.
- Annual turnover: DM1.3 billion.
- Münchners are the world's largest consumers of beer, downing an annual 42 gallons per head.

A CHRONOLOGY

777	First recorded mention of Munichen ("the home of monks").
1158	Henry the Lion founds the city of Munich.
1180	Bavaria becomes the territory of the Wittelsbach rulers.
1327	Munich falls victim to a devastating fire (also in 1418, 1432, and 1590).
1328	Ludwig IV "the Bavarian" is made Holy Roman Emperor and Munich becomes temporarily the imperial capital.
1505	Munich becomes the capital of Bavaria.
1618–1648	Gustav Adolph of Sweden occupies Munich in the Thirty Years' War.
1634	The plague reduces Munich's population by one third to 9,000.
1806	Bavaria becomes a kingdom.
1810	A horse race to celebrate the marriage of Crown Prince Ludwig starts the tradition of the Oktoberfest.
1825–1848	King Ludwig I tranforms Munich into the Athens on the Isar, a flourishing center of art and learning, and a university city.
1848	Ludwig I abdicates following political unrest and an affair with dancer Lola Montez.
1864	Richard Wagner moves here under the patronage of King Ludwig II.
1876	First trams run in Munich.
1886	Ludwig II is certified insane and later found mysteriously drowned in Lake Starnberg.
1900	Munich becomes a center of the Jugendstil (Art Nouveau) movement.

1918	King Ludwig III is deposed in the Bavarian Revolution, led by Kurt Eisner, Bavaria's first prime minister.
1919	Eisner's assassination in Munich leads to the establishment of a soviet-style republic and its bloody defeat in May.
1923	Hitler's *putsch* fails.
1933	Hitler comes to power.
1939	World War II commences.
1940	First air attack on Munich (there are another 70 before 1945).
1945	American troops take Munich. Half its buildings are destroyed and rebuilding begins.
1946	Munich becomes the capital of the Free State of Bavaria.
1965–1972	Construction of the U- and S-Bahn network.
1972	A terrorist attack ends the 20th summer Olympic Games in tragedy.
1980	A bomb attack during the Oktoberfest claims 12 lives.
1990	Reunification of Germany enables many emigrants from eastern Europe and the former G.D.R. to settle in Munich.
1992	World Economic Summit Meeting in Munich. The new airport is opened. Over 400,000 people participate in Germany's first *Lichterkette* (candle vigils) in Munich.
1995	City councils start discussions (Perspektive München) on city development.
2001	Discussions continue over the rebuilding of the Olympic Stadium prior to the opening game of the football World Cup in 2006.

PEOPLE & EVENTS FROM HISTORY

Cartoon of Richard Strauss, one of the world's most popular composers

Thomas Mann's shining city

"München leuchtete" ("Munich shone"), the opening words of *Gladius Dei* (1902) by Thomas Mann, is without doubt one of Munich's most famous quotations. Mann, a resident of Munich, became one of Germany's most celebrated writers, receiving the Nobel Prize for Literature in 1929. Today, Munich remains Mann's shining city, his words stamped on its medal of honor "Munich shines —on Munich's friends."

RICHARD STRAUSS

Munich's greatest composer Richard Strauss was born in 1864, and eventually became the city's Kapellmeister (musical director). The breathtaking Bavarian scenery held a magnetic attraction for him, influencing his compositions considerably, and was particularly evident in his *Alpensinfonie*. His operas are still among the world's most popular and a fountain, depicting scenes from *Salome*, stands in the city center as a memorial.

LUDWIG II

Although King Ludwig II's extravagant fairy-tale castles were a drain on the regency's treasury at the time, they have become the most popular and profitable visitor attractions in Bavaria (► 20). Since childhood, Ludwig had a passion for German legend as epitomised in the operas of Richard Wagner. Following a performance of *Lohengrin*, Ludwig became an enthusiastic Wagner admirer and patron, and the composer's works inspired Ludwig's eccentric building plans. He increasingly neglected state affairs, was eventually declared insane and, shortly after that, met a mysterious watery death on the eastern shore of Lake Starnberg.

ADOLF HITLER & THE BEER HALL PUTSCH

Hitler once said "Munich is the city closest to my heart. Here as a young man, as a soldier and as a politician I made my start." He made his first bid for power here in 1923; the famous Beer Hall Putsch launched his career as leader of the Nazi party. It began when he stormed a meeting of local dignitaries in the Bürgerbräukeller and ended in bloodshed at Odeonsplatz, after which he was sent to prison. Here he wrote *Mein Kampf* (*My Struggle*). Following his release nine months later, Hitler was undeterred. He continued to gather followers for his movement, and it gained momentum, enabling him to seize power in 1933.

MUNICH
how to organize your time

ITINERARIES

These four suggested itineraries will help you cover some of Munich's main sights, aided by the excellent transportation system. Use the efficient subway (U-Bahn) and suburban trains (S-Bahn) or, for a more scenic ride, the buses and trams. The city center, however, is best explored on foot.

ITINERARY ONE	THE CITY CENTER
Morning	Take the U- or S-Bahn to Karlsplatz (Stachus) and spend the morning shopping in Munich's pedestrianized downtown. Pause for a coffee in Café Glockenspiel (► 64) in Marienplatz around 11 to watch the famous Glockenspiel in action (► 37). Don't miss the Viktualienmarkt (► 40) and the smart boutiques of Theatinerstrasse, Residenzstrasse, and Maximilianstrasse (► 70).
Lunch	Choose one of Marienplatz's many restaurants and cafés, perhaps the Ratskeller (► 63) under the New Town Hall for lunch.
Afternoon	Head southward to the City Museum (► 35) to discover Munich's history. If you still have presents and souvenirs to buy, you should find something in Sendlingerstrasse, but allow time to visit the magnificent Asamkirche (► 34).

ITINERARY TWO	ART & ANTIQUITIES
Morning	Travel by U-Bahn to Königsplatz where a choice of three museums and galleries awaits you: the Sculpture Museum (Glyptothek ► 30), the State Collection of Antiquities (Staatliche Antikensammlung ► 30), and the City Gallery in the Lenbachhaus (► 29).
Lunch	Walk northward along Barerstrasse for a light lunch in the Brasserie Trzesniewski (► 65), opposite the Neue Pinakothek.
Afternoon	Spend a relaxing afternoon exploring the classical and modern collections of the Alte and Neue Pinakothek galleries (► 31, 32).

ITINERARY THREE	PARKS & PALACES
Morning	Take the U-Bahn to Rotkreuzplatz, then tram 12 to visit Schloss Nymphenburg (► 24). Spend the morning in the gardens and stop for coffee in the Palmenaus Café.
Lunch	Have lunch at Zur Schwaige (► 63) in the south wing of the palace, then return on foot along the Nymphenburg canal and back down Nymphenburger Strasse to Rotkreuzplatz. Alternatively, return to Marienplatz by S-Bahn, stop for lunch in the food hall of Dallmayr (► 72), Munich's finest delicatessen and have a picnic in the pleasant grounds of the Hofgarten (► 41).
Afternoon	Visit the opulent royal Residenz with its 112 rooms crammed full of priceless treasures, and the Cuvilliés Theater (► 42).

ITINERARY FOUR	ANCIENT & MODERN MUNICH
Morning	Travel to Isartor S-Bahn station. Walk along Zweibrückenstrasse toward the river and the Deutsches Museum (► 45).
Lunch	Enjoy a light lunch in the museum restaurant overlooking the River Isar, or grab a snack in the old remodeled railway car there.
Afternoon	You could easily spend all day at the Deutsches Museum. Alternatively, wander along the east bank of the Isar, past the Maximilaneum, home of the Bavarian parliament, and the Angel of Peace statue (Friedensengel ► 58), then carry on your walk westward along Prinzregentenstrasse to admire the treasures of the Bayerisches Nationalmuseum (Bavarian National Museum ► 48). Late afternoon is always a particularly pleasant time to stroll through the English Garden to the Seehaus beer garden (► 47).

WALKS

MUNICH'S OLD TOWN

From Odeonsplatz walk down Brienner-strasse with its expensive antiques shops. After a short distance the elegant Wittelsbacherplatz opens out to the right, with an impressive equestrian statue of Elector Maximilian I. Soon afterward, turn left at Amiraplatz, past the Greek Orthodox Salvatorkirche, and on into Kardinal-Faulhaber-Strasse where the distinctive domes of Frauenkirche tower over its spectacular facades. The Archbishop's Palace at No. 48 has been the residence of the archbishops of Munich and Freising since 1818. Turn into Promenadeplatz, past one of Munich's best hotels, the Bayerische Hof, the Carmelite Church (the earliest baroque church in Munich) on your left and the Dreifaltigkeitskirche (Church of the Holy Trinity) opposite. Pass by Munich's Wittelsbach fountain (1885) at the main road, before turning left toward Mövenpick (► 68), one of the city's finest coffee houses.

Coat of arms on the Archbishop's Palace

After coffee, continue along the main road until Karlsplatz (Stachus). Pass through Karlstor (site of the former west gate to the city) into the pedestrian zone (Neuhauser Strasse). Don't miss Michaelskirche (► 33), designed as a monument to the Counter-Reformation, before turning left along Augustinerstrasse to Munich's cathedral, the Frauenkirche. Return to the main shopping area via Liebfrauenstrasse and on to Marienplatz.

If you're feeling energetic, climb the Peterskirche tower—the view of downtown is worth the effort. Swing round the side of the church to the Viktualienmarkt. Return to Marienplatz and walk up Dienerstrasse for a traditional Bavarian lunch in Spatenhaus (► 63) on Max-Joseph-Platz.

GARDENS & GALLERIES

Walk past the grand Residenz, home to the great Wittelsbach rulers and art collectors for five centuries, toward Odeonsplatz, then head eastward into the enchanting Hofgarten (Court Garden), beautifully laid out with neat flowerbeds and fountains. Cut diagonally across the gardens, past the Staatskanzlei (State Chancellery) building, finished in 1994, and continue down a narrow path alongside the Finance Garden. Cross Von-der-Tann-Strasse by the pedestrian underground crossing to the Haus der Kunst, Munich's impressive modern art gallery, housed in a monumental building of the Third Reich.

The famous English Garden is just a stone's throw from the gallery. Head toward the Monopteros or Lovers' Temple, one of the park's great landmarks, for splendid views of Munich's skyline. Stop at the Chinese Tower, site of Munich's most popular beer garden, for light refreshment, then leave the English Garden in a westerly direction via Veterinärstrasse until you reach the University, marked by two magnificent bowl fountains. Turn left onto Ludwigstrasse, a grand avenue laid out by Ludwig I to display the wealth of his flourishing kingdom. The Ludwigskirche (Ludwig's Church) on your left contains one of the world's largest frescoes.

Cross Ludwigstrasse across from the church onto Schellingstrasse, just one of the maze of streets behind the university, bursting with student life in its numerous bars and cafés, design stores and bookstores. A left turn at Barerstrasse leads to Munich's two other great galleries; the New Picture Gallery (Neue Pinakothek) with its extensive 19th- and early 20th-century collections, followed by the Old Picture Gallery (Alte Pinakothek), one of the world's greatest galleries of Old Master paintings.

The Chinese Tower in the English Garden

THE SIGHTS

- Residenz (➤ 42)
- Odeonsplatz (➤ 41)
- Hofgarten (➤ 41)
- Haus der Kunst (➤ 46)
- Englischer Garten (➤ 47)
- Ludwigskirche (➤ 57)
- Neue Pinakothek (➤ 32)
- Alte Pinakothek (➤ 31)

INFORMATION

Distance 2½ miles
Time 2 hours
Start point Max-Joseph-Platz
✚ N24
Ⓤ U-Bahn Odeonsplatz
End point Alte Pinakothek
✚ M23
Ⓣ Tram 27

17

EVENING STROLLS

Window shopping in Marienplatz

SCHWABING

Schwabing, focal point of Munich's fashion scene by day, becomes a riot of cafés and restaurants frequented by a trendy international crowd by night. To check out some of the best nightspots, start the evening at Münchener Freiheit and walk southward along Leopoldstrasse. This is the place to see and be seen, with ice-cream parlors and cafés spilling out onto broad terraces. It feels almost Italian. Turn right before Ludwig I's Victory Arch onto Akademiestrasse then left onto Amalienstrasse, where the streets buzz with life. Continue briefly along Theresienstrasse before turning up Türkenstrasse, one of Schwabing's most lively streets, as far as Georgenstrasse. The cozy Georgenhof restaurant at the intersection, with its open fires and wholesome cooking, is a perfect way to complete the evening.

ROYAL MUNICH

Just behind Marienplatz lies a maze of narrow little streets that have retained their medieval character. Immediately in front of the Old Town Hall, go down Burgstrasse, the oldest street in the city, past the homes of former residents, Mozart and Cuvilliés. Continue through the archway of the old royal residence (Alter Hof), then right past the Central Mint (Münzhof) along Pfisterstrasse to the royal brewery, Hofbräuhaus (➤ 43). Turn left up toward the bright lights and dazzling designer windows of the exclusive Maximilianstrasse, then left toward the magnificently illuminated Nationaltheater (➤ 44). Head back along Dienerstrasse, past the former royal delicatessen, Dallmayr (➤ 72), to Marienplatz. If you resisted a drink at the Hofbräuhaus, stop at the tiny Jodler Wirt (➤ 78) one of the most atmospheric, and typically Bavarian watering-holes.

INFORMATION

Schwabing
Distance 2 miles
Time 1–1½ hours
Start point Münchener Freiheit
🚌 L24
🚇 U-Bahn Münchener Freiheit
End point Georgenhof Restaurant, Georgenstrasse (➤ 63)
🚌 L24
🚇 U- and S-Bahn Giselastrasse

Royal Munich
Distance ½ mile
Time 30–45 minutes
Start and end point Marienplatz
🚌 N23
🚇 U- and S-Bahn Marienplatz

Safety
Munich is essentially safe at night. However, as with most large cities, it is advisable to be on guard always and to keep to well-populated areas.

ORGANIZED SIGHTSEEING

ON FOOT & BY BUS

MUNICH TOURIST OFFICE
A range of tours provide a thorough survey of the Bavarian metropolis. Also custom tours (minimum 2 hours).
✉ Sendlingerstrasse 1 ☎ 2 33 30–234

MÜNCHENER STADT-RUNDFAHRTEN
Special tours include *Munich by Night* and city tours combined with the Bavaria Film Studios or the Olympiapark.
✉ Arnulfstrasse 8 ☎ 55 62 89 95

STATTREISEN MÜNCHEN
A variety of specialist walking tours including *National Socialism and Resistance* detailing Munich's development as a Nazi capital; *Hops and Malt* explaining why Munich promotes itself as the Beer City; *Salt & Chips*, looking at Munich industry; and *Schwabing*, exploring the city's intellectual, artistic heart.
✉ Frauenlobstrasse 24 ☎ 54 40 42 30

BY BIKE

CITYHOPPER TOUREN
Choose between two bike tours: the 2-hour *Old Town Tour* or the 4-hour *Romantic Tour* which takes you through Munich's main parks.
✉ Hohenzollernstrasse 95 ☎ 272 11 31

SPURWECHSEL
Bike tours with political or historical themes; also a "green" tour.
☎ 69 24 699

BY TRAM

STATTREISEN MÜNCHEN
Explore Munich by tram.
✉ Frauenlobstrassse 24 ☎ 54 40 42 30

The Hofbräuhaus, Munich's best-known beer hall

Out-of-town excursions

A number of tour operators offer excursions to nearby visitor attractions including day-trips to Neuschwanstein (➤ 20), Zugspitze (Germany's highest mountain), Berchtesgaden, and Salzburg. Contact Bavarian Travel Bureau (☎ 55 14 01 00), Panorama Tours (☎ 54 90 75 60), or Autobus Oberbayern (☎ 32 30 40).

EXCURSIONS

Neuschwanstein Castle

NEUSCHWANSTEIN

This fairy-tale castle is a magical white-turreted affair nestled in a pine forest in the foothills of the Bavarian Alps. In an attempt to make the fantasy world of Wagnerian opera a reality, "Mad" King Ludwig commissioned a stage designer rather than an architect to design this romantic, theatrical castle, and watched it being built by telescope from his father's neighboring castle of Hohenschwangau. Only 15 of the 65 rooms were finished, and Ludwig had only spent a few days there before he was dethroned (► 12). Fortunately, Ludwig's request to destroy the castle on his death was ignored and today it is Bavaria's number-one visitor attraction, and the lavish interior is worth lining up for, with its extravagant decor and vast wall paintings of Wagnerian scenes.

AUGSBURG

Augsburg, one of Germany's oldest cities, was founded in 15BC as *Augusta Vindelicorum* but had its heyday during the Renaissance as one of Europe's richest cultural centers. Today, this lively university town, Bavaria's third-largest city, offers a fine array of impressive Renaissance buildings, including the palace and chapel of the wealthy Fugger family and the Fuggerei, eight streets of gabled houses built in 1519 to house the town's poor, where citizens in need are still housed. Other Augsburg celebrities include Martin Luther; the city played a vital role in the Reformation with its unique "double" churches. Mozart's father and Bertolt Brecht were both born here, and Rudolf Diesel invented the fuel engine here in 1897.

BAD TÖLZ

The beautiful spa town of Bad Tölz, at the foot of the Bavarian Alps, is famous for its iodine-rich springs and peat baths. The traffic-free cobbled main street—Marktstrasse—lined with handsome pastel-colored houses ornately decorated with murals, leads up to the twin-spired Kreuzkirche noted for its Leonhard chapel. Every year on St. Leonhard's Day (November 6), locals bring their horses here to be blessed by the patron saint of animals in an entertaining festival called the Leonhard Ride.

Bad Tölz makes a perfect base for mountain walks, skiing, and other outdoor activities. The nearby Blombergbahn is Germany's longest summer toboggan run and scene in winter of a crazy sled-flying competition, which attracts thousands of spectators.

CHIEMSEE

Locally called the "Bavarian Sea," Chiemsee is the largest of the Bavarian lakes. Its lush scenery and picture-postcard alpine backdrop has attracted artists for centuries and today draws vacationers from all over Germany and beyond to its shores for swimming, sailing and other pusuits.

Take a boat trip from Prien, the largest and loveliest town on the lake, and explore the Herreninsel and Fraueninsel (Men's Island and Women's Island), named for their 8th-century Benedictine monastery and nunnery. However, the lake's main attraction is Herrenchiemsee, site of Ludwig II's most ambitious palace—a replica of the Château of Versailles. Only the central wing of the building was completed, including the spectacular Hall of Mirrors.

INFORMATION

Bad Tölz
Distance 25 miles
Journey time 1 hour
- 🚆 Hourly trains from the main station
- ➕ Off map to south
- ℹ️ Ludwigstrasse 1
  ☎ (08041) 70071

Chiemsee
Distance 50 miles
Journey time 1 hour
- 🏰 Guided palace tours 9–6 (summer), 9:40–4 (winter)
- 🚆 Frequent trains to Prien from the main station
- ➕ Off map to southeast
- ℹ️ Alte Rathausstrasse 11, Prien am Chiemsee
  ☎ (08051) 69050 and (08051) 6090 (for ferry information)

Schloss Herrenchiemsee

WHAT'S ON

Over 100 days a year are officially devoted to processions, parties, and festivals. You can find details in the Tourist Office's *Official Monthly Calendar of Events* or the monthly English-language magazine *Munich Found*.

February	*Fasching*: High-point of the carnival season which begins each November (▶ 52).
March	*Starkbierzeit*: Strong beer season (▶ 52).
April	*Spring Festival*: A two-week-long mini-Oktoberfest at the Theresienwiese. *Ballet Festival Week*. *Auer Mai Dult*: The first of three annual fairs and flea markets.
May	*May Day* (May 1): Traditional dancing takes place around the maypole at the Viktualienmarkt. *Maibockzeit*: A season of special strong lagers, originating from North Germany. *Corpus Christi* (Thursday after Trinity): This magnificent Catholic procession has been taking place ever since 1343.
June	*Spargelzeit*: Celebrates the many ways there are to serve asparagus. *Founding of Munich* (June 14): Marienplatz to Odeonsplatz the streets fill with music, street theater and refreshment stalls. *Film Festival*: A week of international cinematic art ends the month. *Tollwood Festival*: The Olympiapark hosts an alternative festival of rock, jazz, cabaret, food, and folklore.
July	*Opera Festival*: The climax of Munich's cultural year. *Jacobi Dult*: The second annual *Dult*. *Kocherlball*: A traditional workers' ball at 6AM in the English Garden.
August	*Summer Festival*: Two weeks of fireworks and festivities in the Olympiapark.
September	*Oktoberfest* (▶ 52): The world's largest beer festival.
October	*Kirchweih Dult*: The third annual *Dult*. *German Art and Antiques Fair*.
November	*Compaq Grand Slam Cup* (mid-November): One of the most glamorous events in international tennis.
December	*Christkindlmarkt* (▶ 52): Christmas market.

MUNICH's
top 25 sights

The sights are shown on the maps on the inside front cover and inside back cover, numbered **1–25** *from west to east across the city*

SCHLOSS NYMPHENBURG

HIGHLIGHTS

- Amalienburg
- Badenburg
- Gallery of Beauties
- Porcelain Museum
- Magdalenenklause
- Marstallmuseum
- Botanical Garden

Ornate coachwork in the Marstallmuseum

INFORMATION

- L18–19
- 17 90 80
- Palace daily 10–4. Gardens daily 7–dusk. Botanical Gardens Oct–Mar: daily 9–4:30; Apr–Sep: daily 9–6
- Café Palmenhaus
- U-Bahn Rotkreuzplatz
- 41; tram 12, 17
- None
- Moderate
- Museum Mensch und Natur (➤ 60)

It is hard to believe that one of Germany's largest baroque palaces, set in magnificent parkland, started life as a modest summer villa. This arcadian corner of Munich is one of the city's loveliest areas.

The palace Five generations of Bavarian royalty were involved in the construction of this vast palace, starting with Elector Ferdinand Maria. Thrilled by the birth of his heir Max Emanuel, he had the central section built in the style of an Italian villa by Agostino Barelli (1664–74) for his wife. Each succeeding ruler added to the building, resulting in a majestic, semicircular construction, stretching 550 yards from one wing to the other.

The interior The central structure contains sumptuous galleries, including the majestic rococo Stone Hall and Ludwig I's Gallery of Beauties, featuring 36 Munich ladies, some said to have been the king's mistresses. In the old stables, the Marstallmuseum displays a dazzling collection of state carriages and sleighs that recalls the heyday of the Wittelsbach family, and the Porcelain Museum provides a comprehensive history of the famous Nymphenburg porcelain factory since its foundation in 1761.

Park and pavilions Originally in Italian, the park was redone in French baroque style. Then, in 1803, Ludwig von Sckell transformed the gardens into an English park with ornate waterways, statues, pavilions, and a maze. You can see yourself reflected 10-fold in the Amalienburg hunting lodge Hall of Mirrors; and visit the Magdalenenklause hermitage, as well as the Badenburg, said to be Europe's first post-Roman heated pool.

OLYMPIAPARK

Since the 1972 Olympics the park, with its intriguing skyline, has become one of the city's landmarks. Its tower offers an unforgettable view of Munich and the Alps.

The Games The historic Oberwiesenfeld was a former royal Bavarian parade ground north of downtown. In 1909 the world's first airship landed here, and from 1925 until 1939 it was Munich's airport. Used as a dump during World War II, it was transformed in 1968 into a multifunctional sport and recreation area. In 1972, it was the site of the 20th summer Olympic Games.

The buildings The television tower here, now called the Olympiaturm, built between 1965 and 1968, is the tallest reinforced concrete construction in Europe, and has become a symbol of modern Munich. When the weather is clear, the viewing platform and revolving restaurant give a breathtaking panorama of the Alps; the view of the city at night is magical. The tower's futuristic tent-roof looks like an immense spider's web; built at a cost of DM168 million, it is one of the most expensive roofs in the world. When you tour the area on a little train you will see the Olympiasee, a huge artificial lake; the Olympiaberg, a 174-foot hill constructed from wartime rubble; the quaint Russian Orthodox chapel built by Father Timothy, a Russian recluse, beautifully decorated inside with thousands of pieces of silver paper; and the Olympic Village, remembered sadly today as the scene of the terrorist attack on 11 Israeli athletes on September 5, 1972.

DID YOU KNOW?

- The Olympic park covers more than 1 sq mile
- The Olympiaturm is 950 feet high
- The Olympic Stadium, home to FC Bayern soccer club (➤ 83), holds 70,000 people
- The Olympic village houses around 9,000 people

INFORMATION

- ✚ J/K22
- ✉ Spiridon-Louis-Ring 21
- ☎ 30 67 27 07
- 🕐 Olympiaturm 9–midnight. Olympiastadion Nov–Mar daily 9–4:30; Apr–Oct: daily 8:30–6
- 🍴 Revolving restaurant
- Ⓤ U-Bahn Olympiazentrum
- 🚌 36, 41, 43, 81, 136, 184
- ↔ BMW-Museum (➤ 26)

The Olympiaturm

3

BMW-MUSEUM

HIGHLIGHTS

- 1898 Wartburg Motor Wagon
- 1928 Dixi 2-seater
- 1923 R32 motorcycle
- 1935 roadster
- Hands-on "Design your own car"
- Hands-on computerized car models
- BMW 850I hologram—the world's largest hologram
- Movie "The Best is Yet to Come"

INFORMATION

- J22
- Petuelring 130
- 38 22 56 52
- Daily 9–5
- U-Bahn Olympiazentrum, Petuelring
- 36, 41, 43, 81, 84, 136, 184; tram 27
- Excellent
- Moderate
- Olympiapark (➤ 25)
- Special guide in English for children aged eight and over. Phone in advance for a factory tour

Even if the world of automobiles doesn't interest you, it's hard not to marvel at the developments of transportation technology over the past five generations presented at this institution, the most popular company museum in Germany.

The museum The BMW Time Horizon Museum, housed in a silvery, windowless half sphere, provides an eye-catching contrast to the adjacent high-rise headquarters of the Bavarian Motor Works (➤ 59) and its surrounding factory buildings. Over a quarter of a million visitors come to the BMW-Museum annually to see its fascinating display of very rare cars and motorcycles, but the excellent view it gives of the past through nonstop videos and slide shows, all with English commentary, cover such subjects as changing family life and work conditions, the role of women in industry, and car recycling (in which BMW is at the forefront of development). There are even excerpts of old science fiction movies including *Frankenstein*, *2001*, and George Orwell's *1984*.

Future vision Take a virtual journey, via simulators, into the future with electric or solar-generated hydrogen-drive cars or design your own model and watch it develop step-by-step on computers. Adults and children vie with each other to sit in the cockpit of tomorrow's car and experiment with its highly sophisticated data and information systems. At the museum's movie theater, a love story, "The Best is Yet to Come," takes you from the cars of the 1950s to future BMW ideals. The entire museum visit can be neatly summed up by the company's motto, "Sheer Driving Pleasure."

4

DACHAU

Once people visited here to see the Renaissance château and town. Today Dachau is synonymous with the Nazi reign of terror. The concentration camp, (KZ-Gedenkstätte), has been preserved as a memorial to those who died here.

Summer castle The pretty little town of Dachau, with its 18th-century pastel facades and quaint cobbled streets, is set on the steep bank of the Amper River. The Renaissance castle above the town, was once a summer residence popular among the Munich Royals. Only one wing of the original four survives; it contains a large banquet hall with one of the most exquisitely carved ceilings in Bavaria. Nearby is the Dachauer Moos, a heath area often wreathed in mists, which has a delicate light that is much loved by artists.

The camp Münchners used to come to Dachau to wander its picturesque cobbled streets and visit the castle. But on March 22, 1933, only 50 days after Hitler came to power, Dachau was designated as the site of the first concentration camp of the Third Reich. Although it was not one of the main extermination camps, 31,951 deaths were recorded here between 1933 and 1945. Several of the original buildings have been restored as a memorial, a sobering reminder of the fate of the camp's 206,000 inmates. The museum documents the camp's history and the atrocities that happened here. The gates still bear the bitterly ironic slogan *"Arbeit macht frei"* ("Work makes you free").

INFORMATION

✚ Off map to northwest
Ⓢ S-Bahn Dachau

The concentration camp
✉ Alte Römerstrasse 75
☎ (081 31) 17 41
🕐 Tue–Sun 9–5
🚌 726 or 724 to KZ-Gedenkstätte Haupteingang
♿ Excellent
💶 Free
❓ Documentary film in English 11:30 and 3:30

Memorial to the dead

DEN TOTEN
ZUR EHR
DEN LEBENDEN
ZUR MAHNUNG

5

SCHLEISSHEIM PALACES

These three palaces capture Munich's splendid past. Make sure you see the Great Gallery, the charming French-style gardens and the magnificent display of Meissen porcelain.

INFORMATION

✚ Off map to north
☎ Old Palace 315 52 72;
New and Lustheim 315 87 20
🕐 Old Palace: Tue–Sun 10–5.
New Palace, Lustheim Palace,
Porcelain Museum
Tue–Sun 10–4
🚆 S-Bahn Oberschleissheim
🚌 292
♿ None
💶 Moderate

Meissen chinoiserie, Schloss Lustheim

Old Palace In 1597 Duke Wilhelm V bought a farm to the east of the Dachau moor as a retirement residence. His son, Prince Elector Maximilian I, later transformed it into an Italian-style Renaissance palace, and called it the Altes Schloss Schleissheim. Today it contains part of the Bavarian National Museum, and houses among other things an unusual gallery devoted to international religious folk art.

New Palace The beautiful Neues Schloss, "Versailles of Munich," was commissioned by Prince Elector Max Emanuel II as a summer residence. The largest palace complex of its day, it demonstrated his wealth and power. Despite severe damage during World War II, the sumptuous rococo interior remains largely intact. The Great Gallery, over 197 feet long, contains the Bavarian State Art Collection. One of the most remarkable assemblages of baroque paintings in Europe, it has around a thousand paintings, including masterpieces by Rubens, Titian, Veronese, and van Dyck.

Palace Lustheim Separated from the New Palace by delightful formal gardens and encircled by a decorative canal, Palace Lustheim (Schloss Lustheim) was originally accessible only by boat. Planned as an island of happiness for Max Emanuel's bride Maria Antonia, it now houses Germany's largest collection of Meissen porcelain.

LENBACHHAUS

This beautiful City Gallery displays predominantly 19th- and 20th-century works of art. The tiny formal garden is also a delight—a harmonious blend of modern and classical statuary and fountains.

The Lenbachhaus This charming villa was built in 1887 in Florentine High Renaissance style by Gabriel von Seidl for the "painter prince" Franz von Lenbach, darling of the German aristocracy and the most fashionable Bavarian painter of his day. After his death, it became the property of the city and was converted into the municipal art gallery (Städtische Galerie im Lenbachhaus). A north wing was added in the late 1920s to balance the south wing, where Lenbach's studio was housed. The resulting structure perfectly frames the terrace and ornamental gardens.

The collections The chief objective of the City Gallery is to document the development of painting in Munich from the late Gothic period up to the present day. Munich Romantics and landscape artists, including Spitzweg, Leibl, Defregger, Lenbach, and Corinth are well represented, as is the Jugendstil period. However, it is the paintings by the Munich-based expressionist group known as *Der Blaue Reiter* (Blue Rider) that gained the Lenbachhaus international fame, including over 300 works by Wassily Kandinsky, who founded the movement with Franz Marc. Paul Klee, Gabriele Münter, August Macke, and Alexej von Jawlensky are well represented, and the collection of contemporary art by Anselm Kiefer, Andy Warhol, Roy Lichtenstein, Josef Beuys, and others is dazzling.

HIGHLIGHTS

- Kandinsky collection
- *Der Blaue Reiter* collection
- *Show your Wounds*, Joseph Beuys
- *Blue Horse*, Franz Marc
- Munich Jugendstil collection

The formal Italian garden.
Top: Jawlensky und Werefkin *by Münter*

INFORMATION

- M23
- Luisenstrasse 33
- Tue–Sun 10–6
- Café and garden terrace
- U-Bahn Königsplatz
- Good
- Expensive
- Königsplatz (➤ 30), Alte Pinakothek (➤ 31), Neue Pinakothek (➤ 32)
- *Der Blaue Reiter* guided tours, organized by the Munich Volkshochschule, Sun 11 and 4

29

KÖNIGSPLATZ

INFORMATION

- ✚ M23
- ✉ Königsplatz
- ☎ Glyptothek 286100; Antikensammlung 598359
- 🕐 Glyptothek Tue, Wed, Fri–Sun 10–5; Thu 10–8. Antikensammlung Tue, Thu–Sun 10–5; Wed 10–8
- 🍴 Glyptothek museum café
- Ⓤ U-Bahn Königsplatz
- ♿ Good (Glyptothek); none (Antikensammlung)
- 💰 Moderate
- ↔ Lenbachhaus (➤ 29), Alte Pinakothek (➤ 31), Neue Pinakothek (➤ 32)
- ❓ Free guided tour 6PM Wed at the Antikensammlung and Thu at the Glyptothek

Three immense neo-classical temples flank this spacious, majestic square, nicknamed Athens-on-the-Isar, lending it an air of grandeur reminiscent of an ancient forum.

The Square and the Propyläen Along with the buildings of Ludwigstrasse, Königsplatz represents Ludwig I's greatest contribution to Munich. Laid out by Leo von Klenze, according to plans created by Carl von Fischer, the square took 50 years to complete, from 1812 to 1862. The final building, the Propyläen, modeled on the entrance to the Athenian Acropolis, is the most striking.

Nazi control Between 1933 and 1935, the appearance of Königsplatz was completely transformed. Hitler paved over the grass-covered, tree-lined square and Königsplatz became the National Socialists' "Akropolis Germaniae"—an impressive setting for Nazi rallies. The paving stones have been replaced by broad expanses of lawn, and Königsplatz is serene once again.

Museums The Glyptothek or Sculpture Museum on the north flank of Königsplatz is not only the oldest museum in Munich but also one of the most celebrated neo-classical buildings in Germany. Inside is one of Europe's foremost collections of ancient Greek and Roman sculpture. To the south, the Corinithian-style Staatliche Antikensammlung (State Collection of Antiquities) contains a priceless collection of ancient vases, jewelry, bronzes and terra-cotta sculptures. A highlight of the museum is the exhibition of Athenian theater masks.

ALTE PINAKOTHEK

With its more than 850 Old Master paintings this massive museum, the Old Picture Gallery, is rated alongside the Louvre, the Uffizi, the Prado, and the Metropolitan as one of the world's most important galleries. The Rubens Collection alone is the finest on earth.

Architectural masterpiece The pinnacle of Bavaria's centuries-old dedication to the arts, the gallery was commissioned by Ludwig I and designed by Leo von Klenze to replace the older Kammergalerie in the Residenz, which had become too small for the Royal Collection. Modeled on the Renaissance palaces of Venice, it took ten years to construct and on completion in 1836 was proclaimed a masterpiece—the largest gallery building of its time and a model for other museum buildings in Rome and Brussels. During World War II it was so badly damaged that demolition of the site was contemplated. Restored in the 1950s and given an extensive face-lift in the 1990s, the magnificent gallery provides a wonderful backdrop for one of the world's finest collections of Western paintings.

Priceless treasures All the main schools of European art from the Middle Ages to the beginning of the 19th century are represented, with the emphasis on German, Dutch and Flemish paintings, including works by Dürer, van Dyck and Breughel, and over 100 pieces by Rubens.

HIGHLIGHTS

- *Fool's Paradise*, Pieter Breughel the Elder
- *Four Apostles*, Dürer
- *Adoration of the Magi*, Tiepolo
- *Madonna Tempi*, Raphael
- *The Great Last Judgement*, Rubens
- *The Resurrection*, Rembrandt

INFORMATION

- ✚ M23
- ✉ Barerstrasse 27
- ☎ 23 80 52 16
- 🕐 Tue–Sun 10–5; also Thu 5–10PM
- Ⓡ U-Bahn Königsplatz
- 🚋 Tram 27
- ♿ Very good
- 💷 Inexpensive
- ↔ Neue Pinakothek (➤ 32)

Dürer's Four Apostles

NEUE PINAKOTHEK

- *Ostende*, William Turner
- *Breakfast*, Edouard Manet
- *Vase with Sunflowers* and *View of Arles*, Vincent van Gogh
- *Large Reclining Woman*, Henry Moore

The *Laundress Degas*

INFORMATION

- M23
- Barerstrasse 29
- 23 80 51 95
- Wed–Mon 10–5; Thu 10–10
- Café with terrace
- U-Bahn Königsplatz
- Tram 27
- Very good
- Moderate
- Alte Pinakothek (► 31)

The New Picture Gallery, the largest post-war gallery in Germany, is a shining modern contrast to the Renaissance-style Old Picture Gallery across the road, and houses collections through the 19th and early 20th centuries.

Palazzo Branca As with the Old Picture Gallery (Alte Pinakothek), it was Ludwig I who instigated the building of this gallery as a home for contemporary art in 1846. However, it was damaged extensively during World War II, so a competition was held in 1966 to design a new gallery in the heart of Schwabing, Munich's trendy student quarter.

Successful design The winning entry, by Munich architect Alexander von Branca, was built at a staggering cost of DM105 million and was opened in 1981. The attractive concrete, granite and glass structure, sometimes known as the Palazzo Branca, integrates art deco and postmodernist designs with traditional features in an unusual figure-of-eight formation around two inner courtyards and terraced ponds.

Art treasures The Neue Pinakothek contains over 1,000 paintings, drawings, and sculptures spanning a variety of periods from rococo to Jugendstil, focusing on the development of German art alongside English 19th-century landscapes and portraits, and French Impressionism. You will also find here fine examples of work by all the modern masters embracing expressionism, cubism, constructivism, minimalism, and abstract art, including works by Picasso, Klee, Munch, Braque, and Dalí.

MICHAELSKIRCHE

It is easy to miss the Michaelskirche, hidden amid the smart boutiques and department stores of the main shopping precinct, but behind its striking facade lies the largest Renaissance church north of the Alps.

Eventful construction The Jesuit Church of St. Michael was built at the end of the 16th century by Duke Wilhelm (the Pious) as a monument to the Counter-Reformation. In 1590 disaster struck and the tower collapsed; it was finally consecrated in 1597. Wartime damage has been masterfully repaired, and the vast Renaissance hall with its ornate, barrel-vaulted roof is marvelous indeed.

The facade The bold late-Renaissance facade is unified by the consistency of rounded windows, doorways, and niches. In the true combative spirit of the Counter-Reformation, these niches contain stone figures of the Wittelsbach dukes and emperors—secular defenders of the faith—including a splendid figure of the church's patron, Wilhelm V. The large first-floor niche shows St. Michael triumphing over the devil. The highest niche is reserved for Christ.

Impressive interior A further depiction of the Archangel Michael forms the altarpiece of the soaring, three-story altar erected by Sustris, Dietrich, and Schwarz between 1586 and 1589. However, the most dominant architectural feature is the triumphal arch at the entrance to the choir—echoed in the arches of the transepts, side chapels, and galleries symbolizing the victory of the Counter-Reformation. The Royal Crypt contains the tombs of 41 members of the Wittelsbach family.

Michaelskirche has Europe's widest vault (65 feet) outside of Rome

HIGHLIGHTS

- High Altar
- *St. Michael fighting the Devil*, Christoph Schwarz
- Four bronze reliefs, Hubert Gerhard
- Royal and Jesuit crypts
- Reliquary shrine of saints Cosmos and Damian
- *Mary Magdalen at the feet of Christ Crucified*, Giovanni da Bologna
- *Annunciation*, Peter Candid

INFORMATION

- ✠ N23
- ✉ Neuhauser Strasse 52
- ☎ 231 70 60
- 🕐 Royal Crypt Mon–Fri 10–4:30; Sat 10–1
- Ⓢ U- or S-Bahn Karlsplatz
- ♿ None
- 🚋 Tram 16, 17, 18, 19, 20, 21, 27
- ↔ Frauenkirche (▶ 36)

33

11

ASAMKIRCHE

The Asamkirche may be Munich's finest rococo structure. The narrow but sensational facade provides a mere hint of the sumptuous interior—one of the most lavish works of the celebrated Asam brothers.

The Asam brothers In 1729, master architect and sculptor Ägid Quirin Asam acquired a house in Sendlingerstrasse and built his own private church next door, assisted by his brother, a distinguished fresco artist. For this reason, the Church of St. John Nepomuk, a Bohemian saint popular in 18th-century Bavaria is better known as the Asamkirche. Even though Asam financed the construction, he was forced to open it to the public, and the church was consecrated in 1746. Free from the normal constraints of a patron's demands, the brothers created a dazzling jewel of rococo architecture.

Lavish decoration The unobtrusive marble facade has an unusual plinth of unhewn rocks and a kneeling figure of St. John Nepomuk; upon entering you are immediately struck by the breathtaking opulence of the tiny, dark interior, crammed with sculptures, murals, and gold leaf, and crowned by a magnificent ceiling fresco depicting the life of the saint. The long, narrow nave, with its encircling gallery and projecting molded cornice, carries your eye straight to the glorious two-tiered high altar and shrine of St. John Nepomuk. The gleaming gallery altar, portraying the Trinity and illuminated by an oval window representing the sun, is crowned by Ägid Quirin's *Throne of Mercy*, depicting Christ crucified, in the arms of God, wearing the papal crown.

MÜNCHNER STADTMUSEUM

Munich's unique, lively, eclectic personality is reflected in the diverse nature of the City Museum's collections, which range from weapons, armor, and fashion to fairgrounds, Biedermeier, and films.

City history If your itinerary does not allow enough time to explore all the old parts of the city on foot, head straight to the History of the City section housed on the second floor. You can study Munich's development since the Middle Ages through maps, models, and before-and-after-photographs, which illustrate the devastating effects of World War II bombing.

Unusual collections As the museum is housed in the former city armory, it is only fitting that it should contain one of the largest collections of ancient weaponry in Germany. Other collections worth visiting include fashion from the 18th century to the present day, the second-largest musical instrument collection in Europe, and the Photography and Film Museum, with its fascinating display of ancient cameras and photographs. Don't miss the greatest treasure—Erasmus Grasser's 10 *Morris Dancers* (1480), magnificent examples of late Gothic secular art, originally carved for the Old Town Hall (► 39).

For children of all ages On the fourth floor, everyone loves the Marionette Theater Collection (Münchner Marionettentheater) one of the largest in the world, reflecting Bavaria's importance in the production of glove-puppets, shadow plays, and mechanical toys. The nearby fairground museum is rare and most enjoyable. Look out for the moving King Kong.

HIGHLIGHTS

- History of the City Museum
- Marionette Theater Collection and fairground museum
- Photography and Film Museum

Puppet in the City Museum

INFORMATION

- ✚ N23
- ✉ St.-Jakobs-Platz 1
- ☎ 233 223 70
- 🕐 Tue–Sun 10–6
- 🍴 Café and beer garden
- 🚇 U-Bahn Sendlinger Tor, U- and S-Bahn Marienplatz
- 🚌 52, 56
- ♿ Good
- 💶 Moderate
- ↔ Asamkirche (► 34), Münchner Marionettentheater (► 80)
- ❓ Tours, lectures

FRAUENKIRCHE

HIGHLIGHTS

- Gothic stained-glass windows
- *The Baptism of Christ*, Friedrich Pacher altarpiece
- Jan Polack altar panels
- *The Assumption*, Peter Candid
- St. Lantpert's Chapel with wood figures of apostles and prophets from the workshop of Erasmus Grasser
- Princes' Vault

More than any other building, this massive, late Gothic brick church is a symbol of Munich. Its sturdy twin towers (325 feet and 328 feet high), with their Italian–Renaissance onion domes, dominate the city's skyline.

Munich's cathedral The Frauenkirche, built between 1468 and 1488, has been the cathedral of Southern Bavaria since 1821; today's structure, the largest reconstructed medieval building in Munich, has been rebuilt from the rubble of World War II; however, little remains of the original design except the basic architectural elements and the windows in the choir. Its strength lies in its simplicity and grand proportions.

The Frauenkirche's twin onion-domed spires

Onion domes Thirty years after the church's consecration, the towers were still roofless. In 1524, unique green Italian-Renaissance onion domes were erected as a temporary measure. With this eccentric addition to the structure, the building once provoked an irreverent comparison to a pair of beer mugs with lids. However, the domes became so popular, that they were retained.

The Devil's Footprint A footprint is visible in the stone floor by the entrance. Legend has it that the Devil visited the church and stamped his foot in delight; he saw no windows and assumed that architect Jörg von Halsbach had forgotten to put them in, though the building was flooded with light. Von Halsbach had the last laugh, though. The windows are there, but not visible from the point by the entrance.

INFORMATION

- ✚ N23
- ✉ Frauenplatz 1
- ☎ 29 00 82-0
- ◷ South Tower: Apr–Oct, Mon–Sat 10–5
- Ⓤ U- or S-Bahn Marienplatz
- 🚍 52; tram 19
- ♿ None
- 💷 Inexpensive
- ↔ Neues Rathaus (➤ 37), Spielzeugmuseum (➤ 39)

NEUES RATHAUS

Eleven o'clock is the magic hour in the Marienplatz, for it's then that the world-famous Munich Glockenspiel springs into action on the lavish neo-Gothic facade of the New Town Hall.

Towers and turrets The imposing New Town Hall, seat of the city government for nearly a century, dominates the entire north side of Marienplatz, and is traditionally the scene of tournaments, festivals, and ceremonies. Constructed between 1867 and 1909, it surrounds six courtyards with towers and turrets, sculptures, and gargoyles; its facade is decorated with a profusion of statues of Bavarian dukes, electors, and kings. The neo-Gothic style was still controversial at the time, but the Neues Rathaus has become one of Munich's best-known landmarks.

The Glockenspiel On the main front of the building, figures of Bavarian royalty stand alongside saints and characters from local folklore. The central tower viewing platform offers a fantastic view of downtown, and houses one of the largest Glockenspiels (carillons) in Europe. This massive mechanical clock plays four different tunes on 43 bells while 32 almost life-size carved figures present scenes from Munich's history—among them the jousting match at the marriage of Duke Wilhelm V with Renate of Lorraine in 1568, and the *Schäfflertanz* (Coopers' dance) of 1517, celebrating the end of the Black Death. This dance is still re-enacted in Munich's streets every seven years (next in 2004). Both Glockenspiel events can be seen daily at 11 in the morning, at noon, and at 9 in the evening. The cuckoo that ends the performance never fails to bring a smile.

HIGHLIGHTS

- Glockenspiel
- Facade
- Tower
- Ratskeller (➤ 63)

INFORMATION

- ✚ N24
- ✉ Marienplatz
- ☎ 233 03 00
- 🕐 Tower Mon–Fri 9–7; weekends 10–7
- 🍴 Ratskeller beer hall and restaurant (➤ 63)
- Ⓤ U- or S-Bahn Marienplatz
- 🚌 52
- ♿ Few
- 🎫 Tower: Inexpensive
- ↔ Frauenkirche (➤ 36), Peterskirche (➤ 38), Spielzeugmuseum (➤ 39), Viktualienmarkt (➤ 40)

15

PETERSKIRCHE

Known affectionately to Münchners as "Alter Peter," the city's oldest parish church is immortalized in a traditional song that claims "Until Old Peter's tower falls down, we'll have a good life in Munich town."

Built over time The Peterskirche dates from the foundations of the city itself in 1158, on a slight hill called the Petersbergl, where the monks (who had given their name to Munich) had established a settlement in the 11th century. The original Romanesque structure was expanded in Gothic style, and was remodeled along Renaissance lines in the 17th century. The church is famous for the destructive lantern-dome tower that was created then.

Destruction and rebirth During World War II, the church was almost entirely destroyed. In an attempt to raise money to rebuild it, Bavarian Radio stirred the hearts of the people of Munich by playing only a short-ened version of the "Alter Peter" song, and public donations flowed in. After the tower was completed, in October 1951, the full version was at last heard again.

Bells and a view The most extraordinary feature of the tower is its eight asymmetri-cally placed clock-faces, designed so that, according to Munich comedian Karl Valentin, eight people can tell the time at once. The chimes are renowned and include one of the largest bells in Germany; the best time to hear them is at 3PM on Saturday, when they ring in the Sabbath. The 306-step climb to the viewing platform is rewarded by a dramatic bird's-eye view of Munich with its magnificent Alpine backdrop.

SPIELZEUGMUSEUM

With its turrets and towers, and romantic Gothic facade, Munich's Old Town Hall provides a fairy-tale setting for this nostalgic collection of antique toys. It is one of the city's most popular children's attractions.

Toys galore It's easy to miss the tiny entrance to the Toy Museum, hidden at the foot of the Altes Rathaus' (Old Town Hall) grand Gothic tower of the southeast corner of Marienplatz. From here, a narrow spiral staircase leads up to four floors of neatly arranged European and American toys dating from the last two centuries.

Old and new If you start with the teddy bears, toy soldiers, dolls, and model cars belonging to local caricaturist Ivan Steiger at the top and work your way down, you will trace the history of toys, starting with old dolls, animals, and folk toys dating back to 1780, from Bohemia, Vienna, Russia, and other famous European toy-making centers. Don't miss the folk toys from Berchtesgaden, the world's smallest doll and the celebrated Steiff teddy bears.

Dolls and carousels Lower down the tower, a splendid collection of carousels and steam engines is followed by part of the Hauser-Elastolin archive collection, named after one of Germany's main toy producers, and a series of American toys made famous in Europe in comics, among them Felix the Cat and Humpty Dumpty. The third floor contains a series of sophisticated model train layouts, and the second floor has a fine collection of dolls and dolls' houses. Temporary exhibitions complement the permanent displays and feature specific toys or dolls.

Clock on the Old Town Hall

HIGHLIGHTS

- Steiff teddy bears
- Hauser-Elastolin collection
- Smallest doll in the world
- Jumping jacks from Oberammergau
- Moscovian painted puppets
- Model Zeppelin
- First ever Bakelite toy television

INFORMATION

- ✚ N24
- ✉ Im Alten Rathausturm, Marienplatz
- ☎ 29 40 01
- ⏱ Daily 10–5:30
- Ⓤ U- or S-Bahn Marienplatz
- 🚌 52
- ♿ None
- 💶 Inexpensive
- ↔ Neues Rathaus (➤ 37), Peterskirche (➤ 38), Viktualienmarkt (➤ 40)

VIKTUALIENMARKT

Less than a stone's throw from the cosmopolitan stores of Munich's main pedestrian zone, this bustling open-air food market has retained its traditional atmosphere for centuries.

Viktualienmarkt's
maypole

HIGHLIGHTS

- Valentin-Museum (▶ 55)
- Rottler—over 40 different kinds of potato
- Edgar's Müsli-Eck—muesli dishes (▶ 69)
- Lebkuchen Schmidt—spiced biscuits (▶ 73)
- Münchner Suppenküche— soup kitchen (▶ 69)
- Nordsee—fish snacks (▶ 69)
- Pferdemetzger—specialty horsemeat sausages
- Kräuterstand Freisinger— herbs and spices
- Honighäusl—herbal honey wines

INFORMATION

- ✚ N24
- 🕐 Mon–Fri 7:30–6; Sat 7:30–1
- 🍴 Numerous stands serve hot and cold snack
- Ⓤ U- or S-Bahn Marienplatz
- 🚌 52
- ↔ Neues Rathaus (▶ 37), Peterskirche (▶ 38), Spielzeugmuseum (▶ 39)

A long tradition In 1807 it was decided that the market in Marienplatz had become too small for the rapidly growing trade. So a new Viktualienmarkt was planned for a grassy field outside the city, where livestock grazed and stage-coaches stopped. Today the market is Munich's oldest, largest, and most attractive with its quaint green wooden stalls and colorful striped umbrellas.

Lively The robust market women are famous for the loud and colorful abuse they dish out to their customers. Dare to haggle over the price or quality of their produce and you will be scolded in an earthy Bavarian dialect—you won't understand a word, but you'll have no doubt as to the message. Their goods are superb and the prices high but the variety of fresh produce is vast, ranging from Bavarian blue cheese to Alpine herbs and flowers. Look out for neatly tied bundles of asparagus in spring, and mountains of freshly picked cranberries in summer.

Open-air restaurant Little taverns and stands are dotted around the market. It's well worth your while to stop and try some Bavarian specialties—*Leberkäs* (meat loaf) or a *Brat-* or *Weisswürst* (sausage)—washed down with a typically Bavarian *Weissbier.* A beer garden is set up around a maypole, and there are lively celebrations here on May Day.

ODEONSPLATZ

Monumental buildings steeped in history and tradition surround this spacious square at the start of Munich's two finest boulevards. Rubbing the noses of the lions guarding the entrance to the Residenz is meant to bring good luck.

Grand plan for urban expansion Ludwig I entrusted the layout of Odeonsplatz to Leo von Klenze in the early 19th century; the program was to show off the wealth of his flourishing kingdom. Klenze was passionate about Renaissance Italy, and his designs reflect that. The neo-classical Leuchtenberg-Palais, today the Bavarian Ministry of Finance, was inspired by Rome's Palazzo Farnese, and was the model for other developments along the magnificent Ludwigstrasse.

Bavaria's first baroque building, the striking Theatinerkirche, is here; many think it the most beautiful church in Munich. The most imposing building in Odeonsplatz is the Feldherrnhalle (Military Commanders' Hall), commissioned by Ludwig I as a tribute to the Bavarian army, and adorned with statues of Bavarian generals. Note the faces of the two bronze lions; one is said to be growling at the Residenz while the other, facing the church, remains silent.

The Court Garden The peaceful Hofgarten, a park next to Odeonsplatz, retains its original 17th-century Italian layout and its beautifully tended flowerbeds and fountains. The lovely garden is enclosed on two sides by long arcades housing galleries and cafés, and by the impressive Staatskanzlei building to the east.

HIGHLIGHTS

- Theatinerkirche (➤ 57)
- Feldherrnhalle
- Hofgarten
- Leuchtenberg-Palais
- Odeon
- Ludwig I monument
- Preysing Palais
- Staatskanzlei (➤ 59)

INFORMATION

- ✚ N24
- 🍴 Hofgarten Café
- 🚇 U-Bahn Odeonsplatz
- 🚌 53
- ↔ Residenz (➤ 42), Haus der Kunst (➤ 46), Englischer Garten (➤ 47)

Theatinerkirche, burial place of the Wittelsbachs

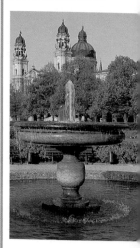

19

RESIDENZ

- Cuvilliés Theater
- Schatzkammer
- Antiquarium
- Ahnengalerie
- Hofkapelle
- Egyptian Art Museum
- Coin Museum

The splendid ceiling of
the Antiquarium

INFORMATION

- ✚ N24
- ✉ Residenzstrasse/Max-
  Joseph-Platz 3
- ☎ 29 06 71
- ◐ Daily 10–4
- Ⓠ U- or S-Bahn Marienplatz,
  U-Bahn Odeonsplatz
- ▭ 53; tram 19
- ♿ Good
- ⊌ Moderate;
  Schatzkammer: Moderate;
  Cuvilliés Theater: Inexpensive
- ⬌ Odeonsplatz (➤ 41),
  Nationaltheater (➤ 44)
- ❓ Tours daily. Separate tour
  for the Schatzkammer

*The glittering state rooms of this magnif-
icent palace demonstrate the power
and wealth of the Wittelsbach dynasty—
five centuries of dukes, prince-electors,
and kings.*

Historical evolution Devastated during
World War II, the Residenz was painstakingly
reconstructed over four decades. Now you
can see it once again in its original state: a
harmonious fusion of Renaissance, baroque,
rococo, and neo-classical styles. Its 112 grand
rooms are crammed with priceless treasures;
as you explore you can trace its architectural
development over the centuries, as well as
the history and lifestyles of the Wittelsbach
family, Bavaria's great dynasty.

Palace highlights It would take a full day to
see everything; if you don't have a lot of time,
just see the Ahnengalerie (Ancestral Portrait
Gallery), hung with paintings of 121
members of the Wittelsbach family; the
Hofkapelle and the Reiche Kapelle, two intimate chapels (one for the courtiers and the
other for the royal family); the Brunnenhof
courtyard with its magnificent fountain; the
unusual shell-encrusted Grottenhof courtyard; and the Antiquarium, the largest
Renaissance vaulted hall in northern Europe.

Jewel in the crown Don't miss the truly
dazzling Cuvilliés Theater, jewel of the
Residenz and the finest rococo theater in the
world. Built in 1750, it hosted the première
of Mozart's *Idomeneo* in 1781. Also, visit the
Treasury (Schatzkammer); the crown jewels
are here, and the collection of ecclesiastical
and secular treasure, spanning a thousand
years, is one of the most valuable in Europe.

HOFBRÄUHAUS

Tourists swarm to this beer hall. Still, it's undoubtedly the city's best-known institution after the Oktoberfest, and no trip to Munich is complete without a visit here.

Royal beer The Hofbräuhaus was founded by Wilhelm V in 1589 to produce a special dark ale for his court because he disliked the expensive local beer. Beer in Bavaria had been considered an aristocratic drink ever since the harsh winters of the 14th century destroyed the Bavarian vineyards. Ordinary Münchners were unable to taste this royal brew until 1828, when the brewery finally became an inn.

The Battle of the Hofbräuhaus After the first mass meeting of the National Socialist Workers' Party (later the Nazi Party) was held in the Hofbräuhaus in 1920, it soon became regarded as the city's most prestigious political beer-hall arena. Here Hitler established himself as a powerful orator and here on November 4, 1921, his storm troops first gained notoriety in a huge brawl, later known as the *Schlacht im Hofbräuhaus*, the Battle of the Hofbräuhaus. Despite the hurling of chairs and beer mugs, Hitler finished his speech.

World's most famous bar Visitors from all over the world come here to raise a glass—or two—or three—at the long tables, and to be served by buxom Dirndl-clad waitresses to the accompaniment of jolly Bavarian music. Everyone joins in to sing the popular drinking song *"In München steht ein Hofbräuhaus, eins, zwei, g'soffa"*..."one, two and down the hatch!"

DID YOU KNOW?

- Munich has the oldest functioning brewery, Freising, in Germany.
- Bavaria contains more than a sixth of the world's 4,000 breweries.
- The Hofbräuhaus is the world's most famous bar.
- The biggest beer gardens in Germany can be found in Munich: the 200-year-old Hirschgarten offers seating for 8,000 guests, the Chinesischer Turm seats 7,000, and the Augustiner-Keller has 5,000 seats.

INFORMATION

- N24
- Am Platzl 9
- 22 16 76
- Daily 9:30–midnight. Brass band from 11 AM
- U- or S-Bahn Marienplatz
- 52; tram 19
- Good

NATIONALTHEATER

HIGHLIGHTS

Outside
- Facade
- Pediment with Apollo and the Muses, Georg Brenninger, 1972
- Pediment with glass mosaic of *Pegasus with the Horae*, Leo Schwanthaler, 19th century

Inside
- Auditorium
- Royal box
- Backstage equipment
- Prompter's box
- Foyer

INFORMATION

- N24
- Max-Joseph-Platz 2
- 21 85 19 20
- Box office Mon–Fri 10–1, 3:30–5:30; Sat 10–12:30
- U- or S-Bahn Marienplatz, U-Bahn Odeonsplatz
- 52, 53; tram 19
- Few
- Tour: expensive
- Odeonsplatz (➤ 41), Residenz (➤ 42)
- Tickets available in advance at the box office (☎ 21 85 19 20) in Maximilianstrasse 11, or from the theater itself one hour before the performance. Guided tours most days at 2PM (except during Aug and Sep)

Munich's Nationaltheater, one of the world's leading opera houses, has been home to the world-famous Bayerische Staatsoper (Bavarian State Opera) for nearly two centuries. It is one of the few German theaters to have been restored to prewar magnificence and is definitely worth a visit.

People's opera-house The Nationaltheater, a distinguished Greek temple of a building with a simple colonnaded facade, stood in ruins for years after wartime bombing until a group of citizens raised sufficient funds, some DM63 million, to restore it to its former glory. It reopened in 1963.

Behind the scenes Most days at 2PM you can get a look backstage on a fascinating tour that shows off the ingenious, high-tech stage machinery. The grandiose auditorium, with five tiers of seating decorated in plush red, gold, ivory, and dove blue, is crowned by an enormous chandelier, which magically disappears into the ceiling when the curtain rises. The impressive Greek-style rooms of the foyer provide an elegant setting for the audience to promenade in their finery.

Opening nights Many important operas have been premièred here over the centuries, including five by Wagner during the reign of Ludwig II, and many eminent people have conducted, directed, and performed here in a repertoire ranging from traditional Munich favorites—Mozart, Wagner, and Strauss—to new commissions from living German composers.

DEUTSCHES MUSEUM

If you spent one minute at each exhibit, it would take you 36 days to see everything at this museum of superlatives—Munich's most famous, Germany's most visited and one of the world's biggest museums of science and technology.

Voyage of discovery In 1903, engineer Oskar von Miller founded the Museum of Masterworks of Science and Technology. Following his death, the collection moved to its present building on its own island on the Isar, east of downtown, and was officially opened in 1925. Over the years it continued to grow and today there are more than 17,000 exhibits ranging from the sundial to the space shuttle.

Learning experience The most popular areas cover mining (the mine reconstructions show realistic working conditions), as well as computer science, telecommunications, and transportation sections. Alongside original artifacts are audio-visual displays, experiments, and hands-on models.

Unique exhibits Some of the most dramatic displays are the star shows at the Planetarium (which takes place in the Forum der Technik), an ear-splitting high voltage demonstration that simulates a 220,000-volt flash of lightning, and the vast model railway on the first floor. Other highlights include the first German submarine; one of the first jet airplanes; Karl Benz's first car; and the bench on which Otto Hahn proved the splitting of the atom.

HIGHLIGHTS

- Planetarium
- Faraday's Cage and high-voltage demonstration
- First German submarine
- Karl Benz's *Automobil Nummer I*
- Copy of the "Puffing Billy" steam train
- Reconstruction of a coalmine
- Reconstruction of the prehistoric caves at Lascaux
- Dornier DO 31 and Junkers JU52 aircraft
- 19th-century sailing ship—197-foot long—the biggest exhibit
- Transport Museum (due to open May 2002)

INFORMATION

- ✚ 024
- ✉ Museumsinsel 1
- ☎ 21 79 433
- 🕐 Daily 9–5
- 🍴 Restaurant, railroad-car café
- 🚉 S-Bahn Isartor
- 🚊 Tram 18
- ♿ Excellent
- 💶 Expensive

45

23

HAUS DER KUNST

This monstrous Nazi building—nick-named the Weisswurst gallery by Hitler's opponents because its crude neo-classical columns look like white sausages—houses one of Germany's finest museums of modern art, the House of Art.

A Hitler project Immediately after seizing power in 1933, Adolf Hitler ordered the construction of a House of German Art (Haus der Kunst). One of the first Nazi architectural projects in the city, it was opened by Joseph Goebbels, Reichsminister of Propaganda, with grand parades of Brownshirts, SS, and Hitler Youth along Prinzregentenstrasse. After proclaiming Munich the capital city of German art, Hitler struck the cornerstone ceremoniously with a silver hammer—which promptly broke.

House of Art At the same time, at the Hofgarten, the notorious exhibit of *Entartete Kunst* (Degenerate Art) was taking place ridiculing contemporary avant-garde artists such as Kell, Dix, and Beckmann who were banned by the Nazi regime. Those degenerate artists continued to paint in secret however, and there is a pleasing irony today that their works are now recognized as being among the great classics of modern art.

Fine art There are no longer any permanent collections in the Haus der Kunst. The paintings of the degenerate artists are now on display in the Neue Pinakothek (➤ 32). However, the east and central sections of the Haus der Kunst, with paintings by Picasso and Munch, remain popular venues for temporary modern art exhibits—both block-buster and more intimate art shows.

ENGLISCHER GARTEN

The 920-acre English Garden, one of every Münchner's favorite spots, is Munich's green lung, stretching over 3 miles along the River Isar. It is one of the largest city parks in the world.

Gathering spot Stroll through the park and you will see people from all walks of life enjoying themselves: families boating, musicians playing, children feeding the ducks, New Age groups gathered by the Love Temple, groups of professionals picnicking together on their lunch break, and jovial crowds drinking beer in the park's three beer gardens. In summer, the park is filled with sunbathers and people wading in the lake.

English influences The English Garden was created by Count Rumford and Ludwig von Sckell in 1789. Breaking away from the French style of manicured lawns and geometrical flowerbeds, they transformed the Wittelsbach hunting ground into an informal, countrified *Volksgarten* (people's park).

Attractions Start at the Kleinhesseloher See, an artificial lake with boats to rent. Or spend time relaxing at the Seehaus beer garden before heading south toward the Monopteros, a circular, Greek-style love temple with a splendid view of the park and the distant spires of old Munich. As well as English and Greek influences, the park also has a distinctive oriental flavor with its Japanese Tea House and Chinese Tower. It also marks the city's most famous beer garden—popular for its brass band, old-fashioned children's merry-go-round, and permanent Oktoberfest atmosphere.

HIGHLIGHTS

- Chinese Tower
- Kleinhesseloher See and Seehaus
- Monopteros
- Japanese Tea House (tea ceremonies on the second weekend of every month between May and October)
- Rumford House

INFORMATION

- M24–H27
- Dawn to dusk
- Chinese Tower beer garden, Seehaus restaurant and beer garden, Japanese Tea House, Aumeister restaurant and beer garden (➤ 50)
- U-Bahn Odeonsplatz, Universität, Giselastrasse, Münchener Freiheit
- 44, 53, 54, 154; tram 17
- Row boats for rent at the Kleinhesseloher See
- Haus der Kunst (➤ 46), Bayerisches Nationalmuseum (➤ 48)

25

BAYERISCHES NATIONALMUSEUM

Top: Riemenschneider woodcarving

HIGHLIGHTS

- Medieval model of Munich, Jakob Sandtner
- Augsburg Weaving Room
- Tilman Riemenschneider sculptures
- Crib collection
- Flanders Tapestry Room
- Weaponry Room
- Closet from Palais Tattenbach
- 14th-century stained-glass windows

INFORMATION

- N25
- Prinzregentenstrasse 3
- 21 12 401
- Tue–Sun 9:30–5
- U-Bahn Lehel
- 53; tram 17
- Good
- Moderate; Sun and public hols free
- Haus der Kunst (➤ 46), Englischer Garten (➤ 47)

48

The Bavarian National Museum is one of Europe's leading folk art museums. The collections provide a comprehensive survey of German cultural history, both sacred and secular, from the early Middle Ages to the present .

Wittelsbach treasures The Wittelsbachs were passionate art collectors. Maximilian II founded this museum to house his acquisitions in 1855. Today's building, on this site since 1900, was designed by Gabriel von Seidl; the architectural style of the various sections cleverly reflects what's inside; the west wing is Romanesque, the east wing Renaissance, the tower baroque, and the west end rococo. There are two main collections— Folklore and Art History.

Bavariana A wonderful series of rooms authentically decorated with rustic Bavarian furniture, glass, pottery, and woodcraft gives you a look at country life of days gone by. The museum is famous for its sculptures by Hans Leinberger, Ignaz Günther, and Tilman Riemenschneider. The museum houses the world's largest collection of Christmas cribs dating from the 18th and 19th centuries, and is split into three parts according to the cribs' origin; Alpine region, Naples, and Sicily.

Art history This series of specialized departments range from tapestries, stained glass, porcelain, and jewelry, to miniatures, armor, and weaponry; the ivory collection is the largest in Europe. You can also see a collection of Bavarian *Trachten* (traditional costumes). And don't miss the model of the medieval city, created by master woodworker Jakob Sandtner, on the second floor.

MUNICH's *best*

BEER HALLS & BEER GARDENS

What to eat and drink

Try some traditional Bavarian *Brotzeit* (snacks, literally "bread time"): *Radi* (large white radishes), *Brez'n* (pretzel bread), *Obatzda* (Camembert and chive spread), *Steckerlfisch* (smoked mackerel), or *Schweinshax'n* (pork knuckles). Wash it all down with a *Maß* (stein) of beer, or have a *Radler* (mixture of beer and lemonade), or a refreshing *Spezi* (cola and lemonade mix).

Enjoying a friendly drink in one of Munich's many beer gardens

See Top 25 Sights for
CHINESE TOWER (ENGLISCHER GARTEN, ➤ 47)
HOFBRÄUHAUS (➤ 43)
SEEHAUS (ENGLISCHER GARTEN, ➤ 47)
VIKTUALIENMARKT (➤ 40)

ALTE VILLA (AMMERSEE, ➤ 53)

AUGUSTINER-KELLER
One of Munich's most traditional beer cellars, just a few minutes' walk from the main station. Its popular beer garden seats over 5,000.
✚ N23 ✉ Arnulfstrasse 52 ☎ 59 43 93 🕔 Daily 10AM–1AM (11:30–9:30 in winter) 🚇 U- or S-Bahn Hauptbahnhof 🚋 Tram 17

AUMEISTER
This former huntsman's lodge, at the northern edge of the English Garden, makes a perfect place to end a pleasant walk along the river.
✚ H26 ✉ Sondermeierstrasse 1 ☎ 32 52 24 🕔 Daily 10AM–11PM 🚇 U-Bahn Freimann

BRÄUSTÜBERL WEIHENSTEPHAN
This former Benedictine monastery in Freising, site of the world's oldest brewery, is famous for its *Korbinian* strong beer.
✚ Off map to north ✉ Weihenstephanbrauerei, Freising ☎ (08161) 53 60 🕔 Daily 9–midnight 🚇 S-Bahn Freising

FLAUCHER
Somewhat off the tourist track, this scenic favorite is next to the River Isar. Families bring their own picnics and candles here in the evening.
✚ Q22 ✉ Isarauen 1 ☎ 723 26 77 🕔 Daily 10AM–11PM 🚇 U-Bahn Brudermühlstrasse

HACKERKELLER
Ox-on-the-spit, the house specialty here, is served to the accompaniment of traditional Bavarian music.

✚ 022 ✉ Theresienhöhe 4 ☎ 50 70 04 🕐 10AM–midnight
🚇 U-Bahn Theresienwiese

HIRSCHGARTEN
Munich's largest beer garden, seating 8,000, is
near Schloss Nymphenburg.
Children love the deer enclosure
and huge park.
✚ M19 ✉ Hirschgartenallee 1 ☎ 17 25 91
🕐 Daily 9AM–11:30PM 🚃 41, 68, 83; tram 17

KLOSTER ANDECHS
(AMMERSEE, ➤ 53)

MATHÄSER BIERSTADT
This typical Munich beer cellar
contains over 4,500 seats, making
it one of the largest bars in the
world.
✚ N23 ✉ Bayerstrasse 5 ☎ 59 28 96
🕐 Daily 8AM–11:30PM 🚇 U- or S-Bahn
Hauptbahnhof

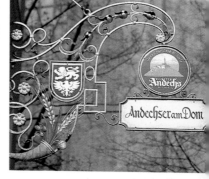

*Bar sign in Munich's old
town*

MAX-EMANUEL-BRAUEREI
Famous for its folk music, this tiny beer garden
near the university is always crowded.
✚ M24 ✉ Adalbertstrasse 33 ☎ 271 51 58 🕐 Daily 10AM–11PM
(evenings only in winter) 🚇 U-Bahn Universität

MENTERSCHWAIGE
Royalty used to drink at this ancient beer garden,
which today serves excellent Bavarian food in a
romantic setting high above the Isar.
✚ T22 ✉ Menterschwaigstrasse 4 ☎ 64 07 32 🕐 Daily
11AM–midnight 🚃 Tram 15, 25

ST EMMERAMSMÜHLE
Largely populated by the smart set, this is the
beer garden in which to see and be seen.
✚ J27 ✉ St Emmeram 41 ☎ 95 39 71 🕐 11–1AM 🚃 37, 88,
89, 188

TAXISGARTEN
This quiet, shady spot near Schloss
Nymphenburg is renowned for its spare ribs.
✚ L21 ✉ Taxisstrasse 12 ☎ 15 68 27 🕐 Daily 11–10:30
🚃 83, 177

WALDWIRTSCHAFT GROSSHESSELOHE
A long time local favorite overlooking the Isar
gorge and famous for its live jazz.
✚ Off map to south ✉ Georg-Kalb-Strasse 3 ☎ 74 99 40 30
🕐 Daily 11–10:30 🚇 S-Bahn Grosshesselohe Isartalbahnhof

WESTPARK–BASTHAUSAM ROSENGARTEN
A lovely, park like place with a hillside view that
takes in thousands of beautiful roses in summer.
✚ 020 ✉ Westpark ☎ 57 50 53 🕐 Daily 10:30AM–midnight
🚇 U-Bahn Westpark 🚃 Tram 18

Bock beer test
In the Hofbräuhaus, that refuge
of Bavarian culture, the "bock
test" was at one time used as a
quality check. Fresh May bock
beer was poured onto a wooden
bench. Hard-headed beer drinkers
would sit on this bench for several
hours, allowing nature to take its
course there and then! If the
bench stuck to their backsides
when they got up, then the beer
was considered good—if not,
then the beer was too thin.

CELEBRATIONS

Beer tent at the Oktoberfest

The first Oktoberfest

Amid the throng, the beermaids, the kaleidoscopic fairground, and the blast of brass bands in the packed beer-tents, it is easy to forget the origin of the Oktoberfest. It all began in 1810 with the wedding party of Crown Prince Ludwig and Princess Theresa—a lavish affair with horseback racing, shooting matches, and a fair, but—ironically—no beer.

FASCHING
Fasching or Carnival—Munich's "fifth season"—officially starts at 11:11AM on November 11, but celebrations don't really get underway until a few weeks before Lent, when costumed revellers run riot in a dazzling array of carnival processions, street parties, and balls, the merriment climaxing with a massive open-air party at the Viktualienmarkt (➤ 40) on Shrove Tuesday.

STARKBIERZEIT (STRONG BEER SEASON)
In the 17th century, Paulaner monks started to brew a special, nourishing beer with an alcoholic content of 6.7 percent, which was consumed as "liquid bread" during Lent. The Pope, not a great beer drinker, pronounced that it was a fitting penance for Lent. The public began to look forward to it each year, and the Strong Beer Festival was born. This unique Munich tradition is best celebrated at the Salvatorkeller am Nockherberg during the three weeks leading up to Easter.

OKTOBERFEST
The world's biggest beer festival commences on the third Saturday in September when the Lord Mayor taps open the first barrel with the cry *"O'zapft is"* ("It's open") and the massive beer binge begins. In 2000, 6.9 million visitors to the festival consumed over a million gallons of beer, 600,000 chickens, and 300,000 sausages.

CHRISTKINDLMARKT (CHRISTMAS MARKET)
During Munich's magical Christmas Market, tiny snowcapped wooden huts cluster around Marienplatz, sparkling with light and crammed with Christmas goodies, tree decorations, and the beautifully carved cribs that are so famous in Bavaria. After buying your stocking stuffers, gather around the enormous, brightly lit Christmas tree for carols, *Glühwein*, and tasty, warm gingerbread.

LAKES

See Top 25 Sights for
KLEINHESSELOHER SEE (ENGLISCHER
GARTEN, ► 47)

AMMERSEE

Ammersee, with its lake promenades, bustling
boat sheds, and sandy beaches, is set in lush
green countryside at the heart of Munich's lake
district, easily reached by S-Bahn. Bavaria's
oldest paddleboat plies the waters and there's an
artists' colony at Diessen, live jazz in the Alte
Villa beer garden at Utting, and Kloster Andechs,
one of Germany's most important pilgrimage
destinations, famous worldwide for its centuries-
old brewing tradition and its *Andechser Bock* beer.
🞑 Off map to southwest 🚋 S-Bahn Herrsching

FELDMOCHINGERSEE

At this beach, the water is so clean you could
almost drink it. For people with disabilities,
there's a machine to raise and lower swimmers
into the water.
🞑 Off map to north 🚋 S-Bahn Feldmoching

FERINGASEE

One of the most popular lakes near the city, it
has sandy beaches, and is good for windsurfing.
🞑 H29 🚋 S-Bahn Unterföhring

KARLSFELDER SEE

A great place for children, with safe swimming
and excellent sports facilities. You might even
catch a glimpse of Emil, the local "Loch Ness"
monster.
🞑 Off map to northwest 🚋 S-Bahn Karlsfeld

STARNBERGER SEE

The baroque palaces of Bavaria's aristocracy line
the banks of the Starnberger See, the largest of
the five lakes just
south of the city, and
the area remains
predominantly the
domain of the rich and
famous. Today, as
Munich's main
summer playground, it
offers horseback
riding, golf, swimming,
and sailing, against a
breathtaking Alpine
backdrop.
🞑 Off map to southwest
🚋 S-Bahn Starnberg

Mysterious phenomena

While the Starnberger See is
famed for its supposed sea
monster—a giant worm, which
agitates the water even when
there isn't a breath of wind—the
Ammersee offers a curious,
inexplicable phenomenon: a
Schaukelwelle (rocking wave) that
crosses the Ammersee from north
to south and back again like a
giant pendulum every 24 minutes,
the water rising and falling about
4 inches against the shore.

Boats for hire on the
Ammersee

MUSEUMS & GALLERIES

Valentin's Day

Karl Valentin (1882–1948), Bavaria's Charlie Chaplin, was loved for his quirky wit and misanthropic humor. Perhaps best remembered for the sketch in which he put fish in a birdcage and birds in an aquarium. He started out in beer halls but soon attracted the attention of Schwabing intellectuals, including dramatist Bertolt Brecht. His statue can be seen today at the Viktualienmarkt (► 40) along with those of other popular folk entertainers.

See Top 25 Sights for
ALTE PINAKOTHEK (► 31)
BAYERISCHES NATIONALMUSEUM (► 48)
BMW-MUSEUM (26)
DACHAU MEMORIAL MUSEUM (► 27)
DEUTSCHES MUSEUM (► 45)
HAUS DER KUNST (► 46)
LENBACHHAUS (► 29)
MÜNCHNER STADTMUSEUM (► 35)
NEUE PINAKOTHEK (► 32)
NYMPHENBURG PORCELAIN MUSEUM (► 24)
SPIELZEUGMUSEUM (► 39)

ALPINE MUSEUM

Everything you want to know about mountaineering in the Alps from 1760 till today, plus occasional temporary exhibits.
✚ N24 ✉ Praterinsel 5 ☎ 211 22 40 🕐 Tue, Wed, Fri 1–6, Thu 1–8 and Sat 10–6 🚇 U- and S-Bahn Isartor 🚋 Tram 17

ERWIN VON KREIBIG GALLERY

Temporary exhibits of promising local artists showcase the latest trends on the Munich art scene.
✚ L19 ✉ Südliches Schlossrondell 1, Schloss Nymphenburg ☎ 178 11 69 🕐 2–5. Closed Mon and Fri 🚋 Tram 12, 17 💶 Inexpensive

FLUGWERFT SCHLEISSHEIM

A must for airplane buffs, this extension of the Deutsches Museum's aviation display is located on a disused airfield.
✚ Off map to north ✉ Effnerstrasse 18 ☎ 315 71 40 🕐 Daily 9–5 🚇 S-Bahn Oberschleissheim 💶 Moderate

GERMAN HUNTING AND FISHING MUSEUM

The most important collection of its kind in Germany, including the Wolpertinger, a "hoax" animal resembling a marmot with webbed feet, antlers, and wings, found only in Bavaria.
✚ N23 ✉ Neuhauser Strasse 21 ☎ 22 05 22 🕐 Daily 9:30–5; Mon and Thu until 9 🚇 U- or S-Bahn Marienplatz 💶 Moderate

GERMAN THEATER MUSEUM

This small but fascinating display of set designs, costumes, photographs, and props brings Germany's rich theatrical past to life.
✚ N24 ✉ Galeriestrasse 4a ☎ 21 06 91 0 🕐 Tue–Sun 10–4 🚇 U-Bahn Odeonsplatz 💶 Moderate

MÜNCHNER FEUERWEHRMUSEUM

Exciting videos demonstrate the latest firefighting methods in this museum. Call before you visit.
✚ 023 ✉ An der Hauptfeuerwache 8 ☎ 23 53 31 86 🕐 Sat 9–4 🚋 Tram 17, 18, 20, 27 🚇 U-Bahn Sendlinger Tor 💶 Free

MUSEUM VILLA STUCK

This stunning Jugendstil house, the former home of Franz von Stuck, has been beautifully restored and contains changing exhibits dedicated to 20th-century art.

🞢 N25 ✉ Prinzregentenstrasse 60 ☎ 45 55 51 25 🕐 Tue–Sun 10–6 🚌 53; tram 18 Ⓤ U-Bahn Prinzregentenplatz 🎟 Inexpensive

PALAEONTOLOGY MUSEUM

Fascinating displays of dinosaurs, fossils, and prehistoric trees.

🞢 M23 ✉ Richard-Wagner-Strasse 10 ☎ 21 80 66 30 🕐 Mon–Thu 8–4; Fri 8–2; first Sun in month 10–4 Ⓤ U-Bahn Königsplatz 🎟 Free

SCHACK-GALERIE

This intimate gallery captures the artistic spirit of 19th-century German art.

🞢 N25 ✉ Prinzregentenstrasse 9 ☎ 238 05 224 🕐 Wed–Mon 10–5 🚌 53; tram 18 Ⓤ U-Bahn Lehel 🎟 Inexpensive

SIEMENS-MUSEUM

Highlights what the future holds in electrical and electronic engineering for the layman.

🞢 N23 ✉ Prannerstrasse 10 ☎ 63 63 26 60 🕐 Mon–Fri 9–5; Sun 10–5; first Tue of each month 10–9 Ⓤ U- or S-Bahn Karlsplatz 🚌 Tram 19 🎟 Free

VALENTIN-MUSEUM

Showcases eccentric humor of Munich's Karl Valentin, with oddities like his first snow sculpture. Even the opening times are odd.

🞢 N24 ✉ Im Isartorturm ☎ 22 32 66 🕐 Mon, Tue, Fri, Sat 11:01–5:29; Sun 10:01–5:29 Ⓢ S-Bahn Isartor 🎟 Inexpensive

ZAM (CENTER FOR EXTRA-ORDINARY MUSEUMS)

The Center for Extraordinary Museums displays collections of chamber pots, pedal cars, padlocks, Easter bunnies, and other miscellaneous objects.

🞢 N24 ✉ Westen-riederstrasse 41 ☎ 290 41 21 🕐 Daily 10–6 Ⓢ S-Bahn Isartor 🎟 Expensive

City of art

Munich claims to be one of the richest European cities of art, thanks largely to the Wittelsbach family, the ambitious rulers of Munich who avidly collected priceless works of art for over 650 years. The majority of the hundred or so museums and galleries in town offer free entrance on Sundays and the Tourist Office produces a useful *Official Monthly Program of Events* with up-to-date information on current exhibits.

Above: Der Olymp, *by Jenssens, New Picture Gallery*

Left: Heilige Barbara, *Bavarian National Museum*

CASTLES & CHURCHES

Lovers' rendezvous

Originally built in 1438 as a love-nest for Agnes Bernauer by her secret lover Duke Albrecht III, Schloss Blutenburg (above) is undeniably romantic. Their romance never flourished: after completion of the magical castle, she was accused of witchcraft and was drowned in the Danube at Straubing.

ASAM-SCHLÖSSL MARIA EINSIEDEL
In the early 18th century this once ordinary house was transformed into a royal country residence with a magnificent façade painted by Cosmas Damian Asam. Today it is a restaurant.
✛ R21 ✉ Benediktbeurer Strasse 19 🍴 Restaurant daily 11AM–midnight 🚇 U-Bahn Thalkirchen

DAMENSTIFTSKIRCHE ST. ANNA
Only the fine facade of St. Anne's survived World War II and the church was rebuilt in the 1950s. The interior, decorated in pastel shades, contains stucco work and frescoes by the Asam brothers.
✛ N23 ✉ Damenstiftstrasse 1 🚇 U- or S-Bahn Karlsplatz

DREIFALTIGKEITSKIRCHE
The Church of the Holy Trinity was built in the early 18th century following the prophecies of a young Munich mystic who claimed that Divine Judgement was about to strike and the city could be saved only if an oath was taken to build a church. Curiously, it was one of the few churches undamaged during World War II.
✛ N23 ✉ Pacellistrasse 6 🚇 U- or S-Bahn Karlsplatz

HEILIGGEISTKIRCHE
The Gothic Church of the Holy Ghost, at the northern end of the Viktualienmarkt, is crammed with religious treasures.
✛ N24 ✉ Tal 77 🚇 U- or S-Bahn Marienplatz

LUDWIGSKIRCHE

Peter Cornelius's *Last Judgement*, the fresco in this elegant church, is the world's largest after Michelangelo's *Last Judgement* in the Sistine Chapel. It took four years to complete.

✚ M24 ✉ Ludwigstrasse 20 🚇 U-Bahn Universität

SCHLOSS BLUTENBURG

An idyllic moated 15th-century castle in Obermenzing. This one-time Wittelsbach summer residence has a chapel full of treasures. It also contains an international collection of children's books—the largest library of youth literature in the world, with over 500,000 books in some 100 different languages.

✚ L16 ✉ Obermenzing ☎ 891 21 10 🕐 Chapel daily 10–5. Library Mon–Thu 9–4:30; Fri until 5:30 🚇 S-Bahn Obermenzing 🎟 Free admission to chapel and library

SCHLOSS DACHAU

Only one wing remains of this popular 16th-century summer residence and hunting ground for Munich royals. Today it contains a folk museum and a café that serves the best pastries in Munich.

✚ Off map to northwest ☎ 08131/87923 🕐 Apr–Sep: daily 9–6; Oct–Mar: daily 10–4 🍴 Café on premises 🚇 S-Bahn Dachau 🎟 Moderate

SCHLOSS FÜRSTENRIED

This baroque castle, scene of King Maximilian II's magnificent hunting parties, is aligned with the Frauenkirche 8 miles away. The wonderful view down the avenue of lime trees is interupted by a highway.

✚ S18 ✉ Forst-Kasten-Allee 🚇 U-Bahn Basler Strasse

SCHLOSS SURESNES

After the collapse of the socialist republic in 1919, this 18th-century summer residence served as a hideaway for the writer and revolutionary Ernst Toller until his arrest here. From then until 1921 it was home to artist Paul Klee.

✚ L24 ✉ Werneckstrasse 24 🚇 U-Bahn Münchener Freiheit

THEATINERKIRCHE

Considered by many to be the most beautiful church in Munich, this brilliant yellow structure is the first example of Bavarian baroque and was an important architectural model for later Bavarian churches.

✚ N24 ✉ Theatinerstrasse 🚇 U-Bahn Odeonsplatz

A birthday church

The Court Church of St. Kajetan was originally built to celebrate the birth of a son and heir to Princess Henriette Adelaide and Elector Ferdinand Maria, and their joy is mirrored in the exuberant interior ornamentation, modeled on that of San Andrea del Valle in Rome. The church was assigned to the monks of the Theatine order, hence the name Theatinerkirche.

The Theatinerkirche

STATUES & FOUNTAINS

A full purse

There was once a fish market next to Konrad Knoll's famous Fish Fountain (1865) in Marienplatz. It then became the scene of the traditional Butcher's Leap where butchers' apprentices were initiated into the profession. Today, they say that if you wash your purse here on Ash Wednesday, it will never be empty. To this day, the Lord Mayor washes the City Purse here every year.

The Brunnenbuberl

See Top 25 Sights for
BRUNNENHOF FOUNTAIN (RESIDENZ, ➤ 42)

ANGEL OF PEACE
This gleaming golden figure, perched high above the River Isar, was built for the 25th anniversary of Germany's victory over France in 1871.
✚ N25 ✉ Prinzregentenstrasse 🚌 53

BRUNNENBUBERL (FOUNTAIN BOY)
Even after public outcry greeted this naked young boy in 1895, sculptor Mathias Gastiner refused to supply a fig leaf.
✚ N23 ✉ Neuhauser Strasse 🚇 U- or S-Bahn Karlsplatz

CATTLE MARKET FOUNTAIN
Three cows mark this ancient marketplace, today a popular picnic spot.
✚ N23 ✉ Rindermarkt 🚇 U- or S-Bahn Marienplatz

MARIENSÄULE
Marienplatz owes its name to this gracious figure of the Virgin Mary. All distances in Bavaria are measured from this point.
✚ N23 ✉ Marienplatz 🚇 U- or S-Bahn Marienplatz

MONUMENT TO MAX-JOSEPH IV
Max Joseph, the first Wittelsbach king, wanted a more dignified standing pose but died before the statue was finished. His son, Ludwig I, settled for this seated version.
✚ N24 ✉ Max-Joseph-Platz 🚇 U- or S-Bahn Marienplatz

PUMUCKL FOUNTAIN
This cheeky character douses passers-by when they least expect it.
✚ K23 ✉ Luitpold Park 🚇 U-Bahn Scheidplatz

STATUE OF BAVARIA
This famous lady representing Bavaria is 60 feet high. Inside, climb the 112 steps to the top for a splendid view.
✚ O22 ✉ Theresienwiese 🚇 U-Bahn Theresienwiese

WALKING MAN
This wacky, 1995 sculpture by American sculptor Jonathan Borofsky is five storys tall.
✚ M24 ✉ Leopoldstrasse 36 🚇 U-Bahn Giselastrasse

WITTELSBACH FOUNTAIN
The two figures of Munich's loveliest neo-classical fountain (1895) symbolize the destructive and healing power of water.
✚ N23 ✉ Lenbachplatz 🚇 U- or S-Bahn Karlsplatz

20TH-CENTURY ARCHITECTURE

BAVARIAN STATE CHANCELLERY

A Renaissance-style arcade frames the gleaming glass and steel Staatskanzlei building with the dome of the former Army Museum as its centerpiece.

➕ N24 ✉ Hofgarten 🚇 U-Bahn Odeonsplatz

BMW HEADQUARTERS

This giant, silver, four-cylinder building looks like a four-leaf clover. It was constructed between 1970 and 1972 by Viennese architect Karl Schwanzer to signal the company's technical orientation.

➕ J23 ✉ Petuelring 130 🚇 U-Bahn Petuelring

JUGENDSTILHAUS AINMILLERSTRASSE

Munich's first Jugendstil house, now restored, dates from 1900.

➕ L24 ✉ Ainmillerstrasse 22 🚇 U-Bahn Giselastrasse

KULTURZENTRUM GASTEIG

This striking combination of red brick and glass contains a concert hall, conservatory, and municipal library.

➕ O25 ✉ Kellerstrasse 2–6 🚇 S-Bahn Isartor

MÜLLERSCHES VOLKSBAD (▶ 82)

MUNICH AIRPORT

Light, space, and movement counterbalance the more functional aspects of this amazing complex.

➕ Off map to northeast ✉ Flughafen 🚇 S-Bahn Flughafen

MUSIKHOCHSCHULE

An enormous underground bunker system built for World War II connects this music academy, designed on Hitler's instruction by Paul Ludwig Troost, to the Haus der Kulturinstitute.

➕ M23 ✉ Arcisstrasse 12 🚇 U-Bahn Königsplatz

POST-UND-WOHNGEBÄUDE

One of Germany's most important buildings from the 1920s, this post office-cum-apartment block has an unusual, elegantly curved facade.

➕ O22 ✉ Goetheplatz 1 🚇 U-Bahn Goetheplatz

Hypo towers

The postwar city contains a remarkable number of modern architectural gems. One of its most original recent wonders—the 375-foot Hypobank headquarters (above)—pierces the skyline in a striking series of shimmering glass and aluminium prisms, each of a different height and size. It was described by designers Walther and Bea Bentz as "white sails billowing between silver masts."

WHAT'S UP FOR KIDS

Munich's very own Hollywood

Kids love directing and starring in their own movies, watching stuntmen in action, and exploring familiar sets (including an entire Berlin street) at the Bavaria Film Studios, location for many famous movies including *Enemy Mine* and *The Never-Ending Story*. Munich has always had strong ties to the film industry, and has a movie Museum (▶ 35), summer Film Festival, European Film College, and a staggering 83 movie theaters (▶ 77).

BAVARIA FILM TOUR
Go behind the scenes of Europe's largest movie studios, and learn the tricks of the trade.
🔟 Off map to south ✉ Bavaria Filmplatz 7 ☎ 64 99 23 04
🕐 Daily 10–3 🚃 Tram 25 💶 Very expensive

BAVARIAN OBSERVATORY
A late-night treat for kids. The staff here will help you find specific stars and comets, and there's also a planetarium.
🔟 P25 ✉ Rosenheimerstrasse 145a ☎ 40 62 39 🕐 Mon–Fri 8PM–10PM 🚇 U-Bahn Karl-Preis-Platz 💶 Moderate

CHILDREN'S THEATERS (▶ 80, 81)

CIRCUS KRONE
Munich's internationally acclaimed circus offers dazzling performances in its permanent big top from December to March.
🔟 M22 ✉ Marsstrasse 43 ☎ 55 81 66 🕐 Telephone for times 🚇 S-Bahn Hackerbrücke

FORUM DER TECHNIK
A high-tech entertainment center containing Germany's first IMAX cinema (▶ 77) and the world's most modern planetarium.
🔟 O24 ✉ Museumsinsel 1 ☎ 2 11 25–1 80 🕐 Daily 9AM–11PM 🚇 S-Bahn Isartor 💶 Expensive

HELLABRUNN ZOO
At the world's first "Geo-Zoo," animals are grouped according to their regions of origin.
🔟 R22 ✉ Tierparkstrasse 30 ☎ 62 50 80 🕐 Apr–Sep: daily 8–6. Oct–Mar: daily 9–5 🚇 U-Bahn Thalkirchen 🚌 52 💶 Moderate

Steiff Teddy Bear (1907), Toy Museum

INTERNATIONAL YOUTH LIBRARY (▶ 57)

MUSEUM MENSCH UND NATUR
The hands-on displays at the Museum of Man and Nature show man's relationship with the natural world in a fun and educational way.
🔟 L19 ✉ Schloss Nymphenburg ☎ 17 64 94 🕐 Tue–Sun 9–5. Closed public holidays 🚌 41; tram 12, 17 💶 Inexpensive

PALAEONTOLOGY MUSEUM (▶ 55)

MUNICH
where to...

Best in Town

Prices

Expect to pay per person for a meal, excluding drink:

$ up to DM25;
 13 euros

$$ DM25–50;
 13–25.5 euros

$$$ over DM50;
 25.5 euros

Dining out

Eating and drinking in Bavaria, and especially in Munich, are major pastimes, with restaurants ranging from Tantris and other gastronomic temples famous throughout Germany to market snack-stalls known as *Imbiss*. Generally speaking, eating out can be expensive, and you need to reserve a table in most places. Restaurants and cafés listed here, like most around town, are open all day unless otherwise stated. Service is usually included in the price, although a small tip is welcomed.

BOGENHAUSER HOF ($$$)

This small countrified restaurant is located in a picture-book traditional house, which stands alone in a pretty garden close to the Maximilaneum. The French cuisine is inspired and the service attentive. A popular haunt for members of Parliament. Reservations are essential.

✚ M25 ✉ Ismaningerstrasse 85 ☎ 98 55 86 🕐 Closed Sun 🚋 Tram 18

GLOCKENBACH ($$$)

Wood-panelled walls are hung with modern art at this esteemed restaurant in the Glockenbach area of the city.

✚ 024 ✉ Kapuzinerstrasse 29 ☎ 53 40 43 🕐 Mon–Sat dinner only 🚇 U-Bahn Goetheplatz

HALALI ($$$)

The secret of Halali's success is its Bavarian style and good, unpretentious, regional home cooking, which includes a range of game dishes. Try the tender venison in a juniper berry sauce with cranberries and wild mushrooms.

✚ M24 ✉ Schönfeldstrasse 22 ☎ 28 59 09 🕐 Mon–Fri lunch and dinner; Sat dinner only 🚇 U-Bahn Odeonsplatz

HILTON GRILL ($$$)

This sophisticated restaurant, overlooking the English Garden, is particularly popular for buisiness lunches.

✚ M25 ✉ Am Tucherpark 7 ☎ 38 45 0 🕐 Lunch and dinner 🚇 U-Bahn Giselastrasse

KÄFER-SCHÄNKE ($$$)

This warren of elegant rooms situated above the famous Käfer delicatessen promises a gastronomic experience with creative dishes and a lavish buffet. A meal here is well worth the expense.

✚ N25 ✉ Schumannstrasse 1 ☎ 416 81 🕐 Mon–Sat noon–midnight 🚇 U-Bahn Prinzregentenplatz

KÖNIGSHOF ($$$)

This gastronomic temple, in one of Munich's finest hotels, offers tempting regional delicacies as well as an extensive wine list in an elegant setting overlooking Karlsplatz.

✚ N23 ✉ Karlsplatz 25 ☎ 55 1 360 🕐 Lunch and dinner 🚇 U- or S-Bahn Karlsplatz

MASSIMILIANO ($$$)

Italian influenced haute cuisine produced with flair and imagination by two young chefs. There is an excellent wine list and al fresco dining in summer.

✚ 025 ✉ Rabistrasse 10 ☎ 448 44 77 🕐 Lunch and dinner 🚇 S-Bahn Rosenheimer Platz

TANTRIS ($$$)

One of Munich's best restaurants, under the guidance of top chef Hans Haas, stands out in Europe for its excellent service and contemporary cuisine.

✚ K24 ✉ Johann-Fichte-Srasse 7 ☎ 36 19 59-0 🕐 Tue–Sat lunch and dinner 🚇 U-Bahn Dietlindenstrasse

BAVARIAN RESTAURANTS

AUGUSTINER GROSSGASTSTÄTTEN ($$)

Beer was brewed here until 1897. Munich's oldest still-standing brewery, now a popular inn, serves reasonably priced Bavarian fare.
➕ N23 ✉ Neuhauser Strasse 27 ☎ 23 18 32 57 🚇 U- or S-Bahn Karlsplatz

GEORGENHOF ($$)

Candles and a fire illuminate this cozy, rustic restaurant. Enjoy the game specialties and tasty apple strudel.
➕ L24 ✉ Friedrichstrasse 1 ☎ 39 31 01 🕐 Daily noon–11PM 🚇 U-Bahn Giselastrasse

HAXENBAUER ($$)

Portions are huge and hearty at this ancient inn. Watch the cooks turning giant shanks of pork (*Schweinshax'n*) over open beechwood fires.
➕ N24 ✉ Sparkassenstrasse ☎ 29 16 21 00 🕐 Daily 11AM–midnight 🚇 U- or S-Bahn Marienplatz

HUNDSKUGEL ($$)

Munich's oldest inn, dating from 1440, takes you back to the Middle Ages.
➕ N23 ✉ Hotterstrasse 18 ☎ 26 42 72 🕐 Daily 10AM–midnight 🚇 U- or S-Bahn Marienplatz

ISARBRÄU ($$)

This remodeled train station brews its own *Weissbier* and has an unusual menu.
➕ Off map to south ✉ Kreuzeckstrasse 23 ☎ 79 89 61 🕐 Daily 10AM–midnight 🚇 S-Bahn Grosshesselohe

NÜRNBERGER BRATWURSTGLÖCKL ($)

This ancient tavern is best known for its Nürnberger Bratwurst (sausages from Nuremberg), which are grilled over an open beechwood fire and served on sauerkraut.
➕ N23 ✉ Frauenplatz 9 ☎ 22 03 85 🕐 10AM–11PM 🚇 U- or S-Bahn Marienplatz

RATSKELLER ($$)

Good food under the vaulted arches of the New Town Hall's cellar.
➕ N23 ✉ Marienplatz 8 ☎ 21 99 89 0 🕐 10AM–midnight 🚇 U- or S-Bahn Marienplatz

SPATENHAUS ($$)

This pleasant spot is across from the opera and popular with the after-theater crowd.
➕ N24 ✉ Residenzstrasse 12 ☎ 290 70 60 🕐 11:30AM–12:30AM 🚇 U- or S-Bahn Marienplatz

WEISSES BRAUHAUS ($)

The *Weisswürste* here is easily the best in town, accompanied by a wickedly strong *Weissbier*.
➕ N24 ✉ Tal 7 ☎ 29 98 75 🕐 8AM–midnight 🚇 U- or S-Bahn Marienplatz

ZUR SCHWAIGE ($$)

The fare is traditional in this café. You can eat in the south wing of Schloss Nymphenburg (▶ 24) or in the shady garden.
➕ L19 ✉ Schloss Nymphenburg ☎ 17 44 21 🕐 Daily 11:30AM–10PM 🚊 Tram 12, 17

Rustic atmosphere

Wooden tables covered with blue-and-white checkered table-cloths, benches, and carved chairs lend a cozy feel to a typical Bavarian restaurant. Murals depicting mountains, lakes, and hunting scenes are hung on the walls next to prized antlers or a collection of beer mugs. Try the *Schweinebraten* (roast pork) with sauerkraut and *knödel* (dumplings) while you soak up the atmosphere.

Sausages

Sausages of every shape, size, and color are undoubtedly the hallmark of the Bavarian diet. The famous Munich *Weisswürste* (white veal sausages flecked with parsley) are served in a tureen of hot water, peeled before eating, and smothered in sweet mustard. Tradition has it that a white sausage mustn't hear the chimes of midday, so everyone crowds the restaurants at 11 to enjoy this local delicacy.
Guten Appetit!

INTERNATIONAL CUISINE

Foreign influences

With one out of five people living in Munich carrying a foreign passport, it is understandable that an impressive array of international specialties is served in the city's 6,000 restaurants. Health-conscious diners have lately been enticed by Asian food, especially Japanese, which is deemed lighter than traditional Bavarian fare. French and Italian cuisine continues to dominate at the upscale restaurants in the city.

AUSTERNKELLER ($$)
Munich's best address for seafood specialties.
✚ N24 ✉ Stollbergstrasse 11 ☎ 29 87 87 🕐 Daily 5PM–11:30PM 🚋 Tram 19

BENJARONG ($$$)
One of Germany's top Thai restaurants, with prices to match, but worth every *pfennig*.
✚ N24 ✉ Falckenbergstrasse 7 ☎ 291 30 55 🕐 Lunch and dinner 🚋 Tram 19

BISTRO TERRINE ($$$)
Exquisite French cuisine in smart art-deco surroundings.
✚ M24 ✉ Amalienstrasse 89 ☎ 28 17 80 🕐 Tue–Fri lunch, Mon–Sat dinner 🚇 U-Bahn Universität

CAFÉ GLOCKENSPIEL ($$$)
One of Munich's most romantic restaurants is across from the city's famous Glockenspiel. There's also a popular café and bar.
✚ N24 ✉ Marienplatz 28 ☎ 26 42 56 🕐 Daily 10AM–1AM 🚇 U- or S-Bahn Marienplatz

CHAO PRAYA ($$)
Make sure you book in advance for this popular Thai restaurant to enjoy an extensive, authentic menu.
✚ M21 ✉ Nymphenburger Strasse 128 ☎ 129 31 90 🕐 Lunch and dinner. Closed Sat lunch 🚇 U-Bahn Rotkreuzplatz

CHURRASCO ($$)
The best steak and salad in town is only a stone's throw from Marineplatz.
✚ N24 ✉ Tal 8 ☎ 29 46 61 🕐 11:30AM–11:30PM 🚇 U- or S-Bahn Marienplatz

DAITOKAI ($$$)
Your personal cook prepares your Japanese meal at your table.
✚ L24 ✉ Kurfürstenstrasse 59 ☎ 271 14 21 🕐 Lunch and dinner. Closed Mon 🚋 Tram 27

ENSHUL ($$$)
The owner of this classy Japanese restaurant starred in the TV series *Shogun*.
✚ M25 ✉ Ismaningerstrasse 136 ☎ 98 75 72 🕐 Mon–Sat lunch 🚋 Tram 18

GRISSINI ($$)
An excellent Italian restaurant, decorated like an Italian palazzo.
✚ K25 ✉ Helmtrudenstrasse 1 ☎ 36 10 12 13 🕐 Lunch and dinner. Closed Sat lunch 🚇 U-Bahn Dietlindenstrasse

JO PEÑA'S ($$)
This Mexican restaurant is always packed because of its delicious *fajitas, burritos,* and *tequilas.*
✚ O24 ✉ Buttermelcherstrasse 17 ☎ 22 64 63 🕐 Dinner only 🚋 Tram 18

KYTARO ($$)
A lively Greek restaurant serving tasty Greek fare.
✚ N25 ✉ Innere Wienerstrasse 36 ☎ 480 11 76 🚋 Tram 18

LA STELLA ($$)
Terrific pizzas draw a young crowd to this excellent pizzeria.
✚ L24 ✉ Hohenstaufenstrasse 2 ☎ 34 17 79 🕐 Tue–Sun lunch and dinner 🚇 U-Bahn Giselastrasse

LE CEZANNE ($$$)
Local fare is the specialty at this tiny, original bistro.
🚇 L24 ✉ Konradstrasse 1 ☎ 39 18 05 🕐 Tue–Sun dinner only 🚇 U-Bahn Giselastrasse

LE GAULOIS ($$)
This restaurant is famous for its fondues.
🚇 K24 ✉ Hörwarthstrasse 4 ☎ 36 74 35 🕐 Dinner only. Closed Sun 🚌 43, 44

LENBACH PALAIS ($$$)
Sir Terence Conran designed this restaurant, one of the most sophisticated in town, on the theme of the Seven Sins.
🚇 N23 ✉ Ottostrasse 6 ☎ 549 130-0 🕐 Lunch and dinner 🚇 U- or S-Bahn Karlsplatz

OSTERIA ($$$)
The wood-paneled dining rooms and subtle decor recreate a timeless elegance of days gone by.
🚇 M23 ✉ Schellingstrasse 62 ☎ 272 03 07 🕐 Closed Sun 🚌 53

PAPATAKIS ($$)
The place to be on weekends if plate-throwing and table-dancing is your scene. The food is Greek.
🚇 L24 ✉ Römerstrasse 15 ☎ 34 13 05 🕐 Dinner only 🚌 33

RUE DES HALLES ($$$)
Sophisticated, Parisian spot in fashionable Haidhausen.
🚇 O25 ✉ Steinstrasse 18 ☎ 48 56 75 🕐 Dinner only 🚇 S-Bahn Rosenheimer Platz

SEOUL ($$)
Munich's only Korean restaurant is in the heart of Schwabing.
🚇 K24 ✉ Leopoldstrasse 122 ☎ 34 81 04 🕐 Lunch and dinner (closed 1st and 3rd Mon of month) 🚇 U-Bahn Münchener Freiheit

SHOYA ($$)
An authentic, yet realistically priced Japanese option. Early reservations are necessary.
🚇 M23 ✉ Gabelsbergerstrasse 85 ☎ 523 62 49 🕐 Dinner only 🚇 U-Bahn Theresienstrasse

TRADER VIC'S ($$$)
A varied menu ranging from Wanton soup to barbecued spare ribs or Calcutta lobster. Come here for great cocktails.
🚇 N23 ✉ Hotel Bayerischer Hof, Promenadeplatz 6 ☎ 22 61 92-94 🕐 Dinner only (until 3AM) 🚇 U- or S-Bahn Marienplatz

TRZESNIEWSKI ($$)
The trendy brasserie of the hour is across from the Neue Pinakothek (New Art Gallery) and is packed from dawn to dusk.
🚇 M23 ✉ Theresienstrasse 72 ☎ 28 23 49 🚊 Tram 27

WERNECKHOF ($$$)
Heavenly French fare on a quiet back street close to the English Garden.
🚇 L24 ✉ Werneckstrasse 11 ☎ 39 99 36 🕐 Closed Sat and Sun lunch 🚇 U-Bahn Giselastrasse

"Mahlzeit!"

Mahlzeiten (mealtimes) are comparatively early in Munich, because most people start work so early (around 7–8AM). Lunch is eaten between 11:30 and 2 and is for many the main meal of the day, followed by a light supper or *Abendbrot* (evening bread). Restaurants usually serve dinner between 6:30 and 11PM. It is polite to wish fellow diners *"Guten Appetit"* then; during the day it is more common to hear the word *"Mahlzeit"*.

VEGETARIAN RESTAURANTS

Vegetarian surprise

Think of Bavarian cuisine and many people conjure up images of enormous roasts and miles of sausages. However, Munich offers some excellent vegetarian restaurants. Their menus are particularly interesting during *Spargelzeit* (Asparagus Season) in May and June when asparagus is served in an amazing variety of ways.

BUXS ($)

You pay by the weight of your plate in this cafeteria-style restaurant, which serves an impressive array of hot and cold dishes.
✠ N24 ✉ Frauenstrasse 9 ☎ 29 19 55 01 🕐 Mon–Fri 11–8; Sat 9–3 🚇 S-Bahn Isartor

CAFÉ IGNAZ ($)

One of Munich's few nonsmoking cafés. This eaterie serves some of the best vegetarian pizzas and risotto in town.
✠ L23 ✉ Georgenstrasse 67 ☎ 271 60 93 🕐 Mon–Fri 8AM–10PM, Sat 9AM–10PM 🚇 U-Bahn Josephsplatz

CAFÉ RUFFINI ($)

The organic vegetarian menu served here is outstanding and the occasional meat dishes are equally good.
✠ L21 ✉ Orffstrasse 22 ☎ 16 11 60 🕐 Tue–Sat 10AM–midnight; Sun 10–6 🚇 U-Bahn Rotkreuzplatz

DAS GOLLIER ($)

A casual, arty place with enterprising cheese dishes. Live music is often performed at night.
✠ N21 ✉ Golierstrasse 83 ☎ 50 16 73 🕐 Daily 11:30AM–3PM, 5PM–midnight. Closed Sat lunch 🚇 U-Bahn Heimeranplatz

GOURMET'S GARDEN ($)

A small vegetarian delicatessen in Schwabing.
✠ L23 ✉ Belgradstrasse 9 ☎ 308 84 93 🕐 Mon–Fri 8:30–8 🚇 33; tram 12, 27

MÖVENPICK MARCHÉ ($)

Although not exclusively vegetarian, the Mövenpick self-service, indoor food market offers a fantastic array of salads, vegetables, and pasta dishes. Save some room for the mouthwatering cakes and pastries.
✠ N23 ✉ Neuhauserstrasse 19 ☎ 23 08 790 🕐 Daily 8AM–11PM 🚇 U- or S-Bahn Marienplatz

MÜNCHNER KARTOFFELHAUS ($)

While not strictly vegetarian, the Munich Potato House offers several delicious meat-free potato dishes.
✠ N24 ✉ Hochbröckenstrasse 3 ☎ 29 63 31 🕐 Mon–Sat noon–11:30PM; Sun 5:30PM–11:30PM 🚇 U- or S-Bahn Marienplatz and Isartor

PRINZ MYSHKIN ($$)

A trendy café with a lengthy menu of creative dishes. Don't miss the tofu stroganoff or the *invlotine*, roulades filled with nuts and tofu. The *malai kofta*, vegetable, ricotta, and nut balls served in a spicy sauce is also very good.
✠ N23 ✉ Hackenstrasse 2 ☎ 26 55 96 🕐 Daily 11AM–12:30AM 🚇 U- or S-Bahn Marienplatz

STRUDELSTUBE ($)

A visit to this take-away strudel shop is a must. The *Topfenstrudel* is particularly tasty.
✠ N24 ✉ Orlandostrasse 4 ☎ 29 85 87 🕐 10:30–8:30 (until 10PM in summer) 🚇 U- or S-Bahn Marienplatz

BREAKFAST CAFÉS

CAFÉ EXTRABLATT
Breakfast until midnight—from *Weisswürste* to bacon and eggs.

🟥 L24 ✉ Leopoldstrasse 7
☎ 33 33 33 Ⓤ U-Bahn Giselastrasse

CAFÉ HAIDHAUSEN
Try the Hangover breakfast or the Romeo and Juliet breakfast for two, served until 4PM.

🟥 025 ✉ Franziskanerstrasse 4 ☎ 688 60 43 Ⓢ S-Bahn Rosenheimer Platz

CAFÉ SCHWABING
Bavarian, French, and Swiss breakfast variations at this trendy café. Excellent coffee.

🟥 L23 ✉ Belgradstrasse 1
☎ 308 88 56 🚌 33; tram 12

CAFÉ WIENER PLATZ
A chic crowd frequents this modern coffeehouse with an extensive breakfast menu.

🟥 N25 ✉ Innere-Wiener-Strasse 48 ☎ 448 94 94
🚌 Tram 19

GÜNTHER MURPHY'S
A popular Irish café specializing in all-you-can-eat Sunday brunches all day long.

🟥 L24 ✉ Nikolaistrasse 9
☎ 39 89 11 Ⓤ U-Bahn Giselastrasse and Münchner Freiheit

KAFFEEHAUS ALTSCHWABING
Enjoy a leisurely breakfast in this elegant café with tasteful Jugendstil decor.

🟥 M23 ✉ Schellingstrasse 56 ☎ 273 10 22 🚌 53; tram 27

MANGOSTIN
The sumptuous Asian Sunday breakfast buffet here is a real treat. Three restaurants (Japanese, Thai, and Colonial style) offer exotic specialties from all over Asia. Even the beer garden serves spring rolls and saté.

✝ R22 ✉ Maria-Einsiedl-Strasse 2 ☎ 723 20 31
🕒 Breakfst buffet Sun only from 11AM. Restaurant also open daily lunch and dinner
Ⓤ U-Bahn Thalkirchen

MÖVENPICK
Munich's biggest breakfast is a 98-foot-long buffet table laden with delicious dishes, in a palatial ballroom. Early reservations are essential.

✝ N23 ✉ Lenbachplatz 8
☎ 54 59 490 🕒 Mon–Sat 8AM–midnight; Sunday 10AM–2:30PM only
Ⓤ U- or S-Bahn Karlsplatz

NEWS BAR
The huge selection of international newspapers and magazines lets you catch up on the news over breakfast in this chic and popular student meeting place.

✝ M24 ✉ Amalienstrasse 55
☎ 28 17 87 Ⓤ U-Bahn Universität

ROXY'S
It's crowded and smoky but very hip and is a great place for people-watching.

✝ L24 ✉ Leopoldstrasse 48
☎ 34 92 92
Ⓤ U-Bahn Giselastrasse

Second helping

As many people in Munich (and elsewhere in Germany) start their working day very early, they usually indulge in a mid-morning snack known as "second breakfast." This may be a sandwich or the traditional local specialty of *weisswürste* (boiled white sausage) and *brezen* (salty bread roll). On leisurely Sunday mornings men often gather at their neighborhood inn for *früschoppen*, a prelunch glass of beer or wine.

TEA, COFFEE & ICE-CREAM CAFÉS

Lebküchen tradition

The 600-year-old tradition of baking Lebküchen is thought to derive from recipes concocted by monks living in a medieval monastery. The cookies, flavored primarily with almonds, honey, and spices, trace their origin back to the honey cakes appreciated by ancient Greeks, Romans, and Egyptians, who regarded honey as a gift of the gods. The pre-Christmas season is the busiest time for Lebküchen producer, Schmidt, when up to three million Lebküchen are made every day.

ADAMELLO

Hidden in a quiet backstreet in Haidhausen, this Italian-run café, named after a mountain in the Dolomites, sells the best ice cream in town. The specialty *Cappa Adamello*— containing a mountain liquor, is delicious.
✚ 025 ✉ Preysingerstrasse 29 ☎ 48 32 83 ◷ Daily 11–10 ☐ Tram 18

ARZMILLER

This popular postshopping haunt can be found in a peaceful courtyard near Odeonsplatz.
✚ N24 ✉ Salvatorstrasse 2, Theatinerhof ☎ 29 42 73 ◷ Shop hours ◉ U-Bahn Odeonsplatz

CAFÉ LUITPOLD PALMENGARTEN

Chic and pricey, this is next to the ornamental fountain in anexclusive shopping arcade.
✚ N24 ✉ Brienner Strasse 11 ☎ 29 28 65 ◷ Mon–Fri 9–8; Sat 8–7 ◉ U-Bahn Odeonsplatz

CAFÉ MÜNCHENER FREIHEIT

One of Munich's top addresses for cakes and confectionery. Pleasant in summer.
✚ L24 ✉ Münchener Freiheit 20 ☎ 34 90 80 ◷ Daily 6:30AM–10PM ◉ U-Bahn Münchener Freiheit

CAFÉ PUCK

A roomy, trendy student haunt in Schwabing.
✚ M24 ✉ Türkenstrasse 33 ☎ 280 22 80 ◷ Daily 9AM–1AM ◉ U-Bahn Universität

HOTEL VIER JAHRESZEITEN

One of Munich's top hotels serves a traditional English afternoon tea.
✚ N24 ✉ Maximilianstrasse 17 ☎ 21 25 0 ◷ From 3PM ◉ U-Bahn Odeonsplatz ☐ Tram 19

MÖVENPICK

One of the city's classic coffeehouses. The ice cream is hard to beat— and scoops are the size of tennis balls.
✚ N23 ✉ Lenbachplatz 8 ☎ 54 5949-0 ◷ Daily 8AM–midnight ◉ U- or S-Bahn Karlsplatz

SARCLETTIS EIS-ECKE

It's the largest ice cream menu in town, with over 100 flavors.
✚ M21 ✉ Nymphenburger Strasse 155 ☎ 15 53 14 ◉ U-Bahn Rotkreuzplatz

SCHLOSS CAFÉ DACHAU

A magnificent palace is the setting for Munich's best gateaux.
✚ Off map to northwest ✉ Schloss Dachau ☎ (08131) 45 43 660 ◷ Daily 10AM–1AM ◉ S-Bahn Dachau

SCHLOSSCAFÉ IM PALMENHAUS

An elegant café in the Nymphenburg Palace's giant palm house.
✚ L19 ✉ Schloss Nymphenburg ☎ 17 53 09 ◷ 10–6 ☐ Tram 12, 17

VENEZIA

The best ice-cream café on Leopoldstrasse.
✚ L24 ✉ Leopoldstrasse 31 ☎ 39 55 40 ◉ U-Bahn Giselastrasse

SNACKS

BERNI'S NEDELBRETT ($)

A cheap, cheerful pasta joint. On Saturdays and Sundays from 8PM, during Pasta Happy Hour, the prices drop 50 percent.

➕ N24 ✉ Petersplatz 8† ☎ 26 44 69 🕐 Sun–Thu 11–10; Fri–Sat 11–11 🚇 U- or S-Bahn Marienplatz 🚋 Tram 27

EDGAR'S MÜSLI-ECK ($)

Edgar's *Birchermüsli* (yoghurt, fruit, and muesli mixtures) are both filling and healthy.

➕ N24 ✉ Viktualienmarkt 🕐 Shop hours 🚇 U- or S-Bahn Marienplatz

MOLLY MALONE ($)

The best fish'n chips shop in town.

➕ O25 ✉ Kellerstrasse 21, Haidhausen ☎ 688 75 10 🕐 Mon–Fri 5PM–1AM; Sat and Sun noon–1AM 🚇 S-Bahn Rosenheimerplatz

MÜNCHNER SUPPENKÜCHE ($)

At this soup kitchen make sure you don't miss the *Pfannekuchensuppe* (pancake soup) or *Leberknödelsuppe* (liver dumpling soup).

➕ N24 ✉ Viktualienmarkt 🕐 Shop hours 🚇 U- or S-Bahn Marienplatz

MUNICH'S FIRST DINER ($)

A roller-skating staff serves burgers and milkshakes at this American-style diner, full of 1950s memorabilia.

➕ L24 ✉ Leopoldstrasse 82 ☎ 33 59 15 🕐 Sun–Thu

7:30AM–1AM; Fri–Sat 7:30AM–1AM 🚇 U-Bahn Münchener Freiheit

NORDSEE ($

This fish seller offers a range of hot and cold dishes. Standing only.

➕ N24 ✉ Viktualienmarkt ☎ 22 11 86 🕐 Mon–Fri 8–7; Sat 8–4 🚇 U- or S-Bahn Marienplatz

TIRAMISU ($)

This tiny Italian bar serves excellent *antipasti* and has an interesting pasta menu that changes daily.

➕ L23 ✉ Hohenzollernstrasse 124 ☎ 308 60 08 🕐 Mon–Fri 11.30–10 🚇 U-Bahn Hohenzollernplatz

VINCENZ MURR ($)

You can help yourself at the extensive salad bar, then have a picnic by the fountain opposite, at Rindermarkt.

➕ N23 ✉ Rosenstrasse 7 ☎ 260 47 65 🕐 Shop hours 🚇 U- or S-Bahn Marienplatz

VINI E PANINI ($)

Not only bread and wine but also snacks from different regions of Italy.

➕ L24 ✉ Nordendstrasse 45 ☎ 2 72 17 43 🕐 Mon–Fri 10–6:30; Sat 10–2 🚋 Tram 27

WOKMAN ($)

Inexpensive and tasty Chinese fast food.

➕ L24 ✉ Leopoldstrasse 68 ☎ 39 03 43 🕐 Daily 11AM–midnight 🚇 U-Bahn Münchener Freiheit

Essential snacks

Any excuse is found for a quick snack or *Brotzeit* (bread time) in Munich, to tide you over until the serious eating begins. The city's countless snackbars (usually called *Kneipe*, *Lokal*, or *Schnellimbiss*) and butchers' shops (*Metzgereien*) often serve such specialties as *Leberkäs* (a meatloaf of beef, pork, and spices), *Kartoffelpuffer* (potato fritters), *Radi* (thin slices of salted horseradish) and, of course, sausages.

SHOPPING AREAS

Bargain-hunting

Munich has over 8,000 stores and 15 big department stores and there are plenty of bargains to be had if you know where to look. Start with the department stores that sell cut-price goods in their basements, and always keep your eyes open for *Sonderangebot* (special offers) signs. As always, the best bargains can be found at the end of season sales in January and July, and the discounts can often be astonishing.

Opening times

Most stores are open weekdays from 9 until 6:30, with late-night shopping (*Stadtabend*) on Thursdays until 8:30. Don't leave it until Saturday to do your trip shopping as most stores close at 1 or 2PM, except on the first Saturday in every month, when they remain open until 4. However, legislation now permits stores to stay open until 8 on weekdays and until 4 on Saturdays, so opening and closing times are changing around town.

ANTIQUES
All over Schwabing there are stores specialising in antiques, in particular English, Jugendstil and art deco. Hunt for bargains in the narrow alleys off Tal and behind the Viktualienmarkt or visit one of the many auction houses around the town.

ARTS & CRAFTS
Browse through Maximilianstrasse's 25 galleries or explore Briennerstrasse, Theatinerstrasse and the arcades of the Hofgarten. For the finest in Bavarian handicrafts, visit the Kunstgewerbe-Verein (▶ 71) in Pacellistrasse or look in the streets converging on Max-Joseph-Platz.

BOOKSTORES
There are a staggering 300 publishing houses in Munich and a wide variety of bookstores concentrated in the city center and also near the university in Schellingstrasse.

FASHION
Boutiques stock everything from *haute couture* to Bavarian folk costume and the most unusual new trends. In the elegant shops of Theatinerstrasse, Residenzstrasse and Maximilianstrasse you will find famous names such as Yves Saint Laurent, Armani and Hermès. Even the small side-streets, with their mazes of attractive arcades and passages leading to Residenzstrasse, are packed with chic designer boutiques. The most popular shopping street is the pedestrian zone between Karlsplatz and Marienplatz, where huge department stores are interspersed with elegant boutiques and everyday stores. In summer you will find buskers and street entertainers every few yards.

The smart shops of Sendlingerstrasse bridge the price gap between the exclusive Maximilianstrasse area and the pedestrian zone; with smart fashions, imaginative gift stores and giant sports and department stores. Head straight to the lively shopping area of Schwabing for creative and stylish clothes to suit every purse. Near the university you can find something really original in the way-out shops and numerous second-hand stores.

INTERIOR DESIGN
Check out Ludwigstrasse, Briennerstrasse and Tal for fine furnishings and designer gadgets.

JEWELRY
Maximilianstrasse has many famous jewelers including Bulgari. Look in Schwabing for more reasonably priced shops.

GIFTS & BAVARIAN SOUVENIRS

ETCETERA

Full of novel Bavarian souvenirs and things you would love to buy but don't really need.

➕ N24 ✉ Wurzerstrasse 12 ☎ 22 60 68 🚇 U- or S-Bahn Marienplatz

GESCHENKE KAISER

Pewter Christmas decorations, serving dishes, candlesticks, and beer jugs.

➕ N24 ✉ Rindermarkt 1 ☎ 26 45 09 🚇 U- or S-Bahn Marienplatz

I-DÜPFERL

Three floors of tempting ideas for vacation gifts, including fun household gadgets and interesting knick-knacks.

➕ N24 ✉ Im Tal 31 ☎ 291 95 70 🚇 S-Bahn Isartor

KUNSTGEWERBE-VEREIN

Shop here for high-quality, carved, painted, and handcrafted Bavarian products. Choose from a variety of puppets and pottery to jewelry and bright carnival masks—truly exclusive gifts.

➕ N23 ✉ Pacellistrasse 6–8 ☎ 290 14 70 🚇 U- or S-Bahn Karlsplatz

LEDERHOSEN WAGNER

This store has been making Bavaria's distinctive leather shorts from soft deerskin since 1825. Surprise your friends with a "shaving brush" hat, made out of chamois hair, to match the shorts.

➕ N24 ✉ Tal 2 ☎ 22 56 97 🚇 U- or S-Bahn Marienplatz

LODEN FREY

The largest folk costume specialist store, *Trachten*, in the world is Munich's top outlet for such outfits, with an almost endless choice of styles. Kids love the toboggan run from the first floor to the basement.

➕ N23 ✉ Maffeistrasse 7–9 ☎ 21 03 90 🚇 U- or S-Bahn Marienplatz

MÜNCHNER GESCHENKE-STUBEN

Crammed with every imaginable Bavarian souvenir.

➕ N24 ✉ Petersplatz 8 ☎ 26 74 56 🚇 U- or S-Bahn Marienplatz

MÜNCHNER MUSIKDOSEN

The traditional musical boxes here make a perfect gift to take home.

➕ N24 ✉ Pfisterstrasse 8 ☎ 290 40 91 🚇 U- or S-Bahn Marienplatz

STOCKHAMMER

Idea-hungry shoppers are sure to find original gifts here.

➕ L24 ✉ Hohenzollernstrasse 33 ☎ 34 77 81 🚇 U- or S-Bahn Münchener Freiheit

WALLACH

This famous rococo-fronted store is full of Bavarian atmosphere and attractive gifts, including fantastic hand-printed fabrics and *Dirndls*.

➕ N24 ✉ Residenzstrasse 3 ☎ 22 08 71 🚇 U- or S-Bahn Marienplatz

Trachten and more

The nice thing about *Trachten* (Bavarian folk costume) is that Münchners really do wear it, especially on Sundays, public holidays, or festive occasions. Most popular are the *Lederhosen* and the sharp green-collared gray jackets for men or the gaily-colored *Dirndl* dresses with fitted bodices and full gathered skirts.

DEPARTMENT STORES, FOOD STORES & MARKETS

BAGEL SHOP
Choose from sesame, garlic, onion, raisin, blueberry, pumpernickel, and plain, with toppings ranging from smoked salmon and sour cream to pastrami and tomato. Also muffins, brownies, and cookies. Delivery.
✚ M23 ✉ Barerstrasse 72 ☎ 271 21 86 🚋 Tram 27

BOETTNER
One of Munich's oldest hostelries is well known for its schnapps, caviare, and other delicacies.
✚ N24 ✉ Theatinerstrasse 8 ☎ 22 12 10 Ⓤ U- or S-Bahn Marienplatz

DALLMAYR
The city's top delicatessen used to supply the Bavarian royal family. The second floor serves a great champagne breakfast.
✚ N24 ✉ Dienerstrasse 14-15 ☎ 213 51 00 Ⓤ U- or S-Bahn Marienplatz

EILLES
One of several Eilles stores, selling fine tea, coffee, and wines.
✚ N24 ✉ Residenzstrasse 13 ☎ 22 61 84 Ⓤ U- or S-Bahn Marienplatz

ELISABETHMARKT
Schwabing's *Viktualienmarkt*, with surprisingly few tourists.
✚ L23 ✉ Elisabethplatz 🚋 Tram 27

ELLY SEIDL
A tiny chocolate shop, famous for its pralines, and its *Münchner Kuppeln* chocolates which look like the onion-domes of the Frauenkirche.

✚ N24 ✉ Am Kosttor 2 ☎ 22 15 22 Ⓤ U- or S-Bahn Marienplatz

HERTIE
This branch of the Hertie department store chain stretches from the main train station to Karlsplatz and offers everyday items at reasonable prices.
✚ N23 ✉ Bahnhofplatz ☎ 551 20 Ⓤ U- or S-Bahn Hauptbahnhof

KÄFER
An epicurean labyrinth selling food and drink from around the world in the fashionable Bogenhausen district.
✚ N25 ✉ Prinzregentenstrasse 73 ☎ 416 81 Ⓤ U-Bahn Prinzregentenplatz

KARSTADT
This giant department store is divided into three: Haus Oberpollinger am Dom sells electical appliances, books, and furnishings; Karstadt am Karlstor offers cosmetics and clothing; Karstadt Sporthaus Oberpollinger stocks sports items.
✚ N23 ✉ Neuhauser Strasse 18 ☎ 29 02 30 Ⓤ U- or S-Bahn Karlsplatz

KAUFHOF
One of several Kaufhof department stores here; centrally located.
✚ N24 ✉ Kaufingerstrasse 2 ☎ 23 18 51 Ⓤ U- or S-Bahn Marienplatz

LA MAISON DU VIN
There is an exceptional range of fine French wines here.

Celebrating in style

When Paul and Elsa Käfer opened a modest food and wine store in Munich in 1930, they had no idea that their name would become synonymous with the stylish parties that their son would arrange, in the more prosperous 1960s, for movie stars and other prominent members of postwar high society. The store survives as a cooks' paradise and the catering side of the business now supplies museums and restaurants including the rooftop restaurant of the renovated German parliament building (Reichstag) in Berlin.

🚇 L24 ✉ Nordendstrasse 62
☎ 272 05 52 🚋 Tram 27

LE CHALET DU FROMAGE

One of Munich's best cheese sellers.
🚇 L24 ✉ Stand 11, Elisabethplatz 🕐 Closed Mon
🚋 Tram 27

LUDWIG BECK

Beck is without doubt Munich's most stylish department store, a Munich institution with a changing decor created by well-known artists. At Christmas, artisans work on the top floor and the store becomes a winter wonderland of handicrafts. Round off your visit with a snack at the oriental Sum Bar.
🚇 N24 ✉ Marienplatz 11
☎ 23 69 10 🚇 U- or S-Bahn Marienplatz

MARKT AM WIENER PLATZ

Tiny green wooden produce stands huddled around the maypole in Haidhausen—an attractive alternative to the supermarket.
🚇 N25 ✉ Wiener Platz
🚇 U-Bahn Max-Weber-Platz

OLYMPIA EINKAUFSZENTRUM (OEZ)

For everything under one roof, visit this massive shopping center with over 100 stores near the Olympiapark.
🚇 H21 ✉ Hanauerstrasse 68
☎ 141 60 02 🚌 36

RISCHART

One of many Rischart stores offers the largest choice of bread, rolls, and cakes in town.
🚇 N24 ✉ Marienplatz 18
☎ 231 70 00 🚇 U- or S-Bahn Marienplatz

SCHMIDT

Shop here for Lebküchen, delicious spice cookies, which are presented in collectable tins, along with *Stollen* (fruitcakes).
🚇 N24 ✉ Westenriederstrasse 8a ☎ 29 50 68 🚇 S-Bahn Isartor

SPANISCHES FRUCHTHAUS

A mouthwatering display of dried fruits entices you into this small store with an unusual selection of crystallized, fresh, and chocolate-coated fruits.
🚇 N23 ✉ Rindermarkt 10
☎ 26 45 70 🚇 U- or S-Bahn Marienplatz

SPORT-SCHECK

The department store for sports fanatics. Six floors are dedicated to every sport imaginable. You can even arrange sporting activities or a day-long ski trip on the seventh floor.
🚇 N23 ✉ Sendlingerstrasse 85 ☎ 21 66 12 54 🚇 U-Bahn Sendlinger Tor

VIKTUALIENMARKT

The largest and most famous Bavarian open-air food market is near the bustling city center. Look out for the Kuterstand Freisinger stand for Alpine herbs and the Honighusl stand for honey products.
🚇 N24 🕐 Mon–Fri 7:30–6; Sat 7:30AM–1PM 🚇 U- or S-Bahn Marienplatz

Flea markets

Flea markets have long been a tradition in Munich, offering fun shopping either in the small impromptu markets or in the large, well-organized, commercial ones in Arnulfstrasse or in the grounds of the Pfanni factory on the east side of Munich. One of Munich's largest and most popular markets takes place on the first day of the *Frühlingsfest* (Spring Festival) in April.

SPECIALIST SHOPS

Handcrafted porcelain

The manufacture of exquisite porcelain figurines and dishes was started 250 years ago by Prince Elector Maximilian III Joseph at his Nymphenburg Palace in suburban Munich. Today, about 85 artists and artisans keep alive traditional methods at a cramped factory across from the palace, throwing, forming, and painting each piece by hand. Their delicate creations range from bowls and cups to graceful dancers and animals.

AGGENTI
The emphasis here is on fun designer gifts and household goods.
✚ N24 ✉ Tal 20 ☎ 29 78 08 🚇 U- or S-Bahn Marienplatz

ANGLIA ENGLISH BOOKSTORE
This store, near the University, claims to have the largest selection of English paperbacks, childrens books, fiction, and non-fiction in Germany.
✚ M24 ✉ Schellingstrasse 3 ☎ 28 36 42 🚇 U-Bahn Universität

DAS LANDHAUSECK
A cornucopia of traditional Bavarian furniture and antiques.
✚ N23 ✉ St Jacobs-Platz 12 ☎ 260 95 72 🚇 U-Bahn Sendlinger Tor

DEHNER
Full of great gift ideas for garden lovers. What about a packet of Alpine flower seeds or even a grow-your-own Bavarian meadow lawn?
✚ N24 ✉ Frauenstrasse 8 ☎ 24 23 99 80 🚇 S-Bahn Isartor

DIE EINRICHTUNG
The interior design store in Munich.
✚ N23 ✉ Briennerstrasse 12 🚇 U-Bahn Odeonsplatz

DIE PUPPENSTUBE
Dolls and puppets to take you back to your childhood.
✚ M23 ✉ Luisenstrasse 68 ☎ 272 32 67 🚌 53

FOURTH DIMENSION
One of Germany's leading costume jewelry stores. Smart but affordable.
✚ N23 ✉ Frauenplatz 14 ☎ 22 80 10 90 🚇 S-Bahn Marienplatz

HEMMERLE
The treasures in this traditional Munich jewelers are expensive but very solid.
✚ N24 ✉ Maximilianstrasse 14 ☎ 24 22 600 🚋 Tram 19

HIEBER AM DOM
One of the best bets in Munich for CDs, tapes, and sheet music.
✚ N23 ✉ Liebfrauenstrasse 1 ☎ 29 00 80 14 🚇 U- or S-Bahn Marienplatz

HUGENDUBEL
Bookworms love this giant book superstore, spread over four floors. There are even sofas where you can sit and read without buying. Several branches throughout Munich.
✚ N24 ✉ Marienplatz 🚇 U- or S-Bahn Marienplatz

KAUT-BULLINGER
Three floors of chic staitonery ranging from pens, writing paper, and art materials to leather personal organizers and designer wrapping paper.
✚ N23 ✉ Rosenstrasse 8 ☎ 23 80 00 🚇 U-or S-Bahn Marienplatz

KUNST UND SPIEL
A magical store full of sturdy, educational toys together with an extensive arts and craft section.
✚ L24 ✉ Leopoldstrasse 48 ☎ 381 62 70 🚇 U-Bahn Giselastrasse

LANDPARTIE

A friendly welcome and a homey atmosphere greet customers at this delightful store, crammed with both antique furniture and interesting household accessories.

🗺 L24 ✉ Kurfürstenstrasse 12 ☎ 34 85 98 🚋 Tram 27

LEUTE – ALLES AUS HOLZ

Everything sold here is made of wood, with a range of decorative and functional items from games to cookie cutters.

🗺 N24 ✉ Viktualienmarkt 15 ☎ 26 82 48 🚇 U- or S-Bahn Marienplatz

OBLETTER

A comprehensive toy store that sells everything from cuddly toys to train sets. Several branches around town.

🗺 N23 ✉ Karlsplatz 11–12 ☎ 55 08 95 10 🚇 U- or S-Bahn Karlsplatz

PERLENMARKT

This unique store sells nothing but buttons, beads, and jewelry-making equipment.

🗺 L24 ✉ Nordendstrasse 28 ☎ 271 05 76 🚋 Tram 27

PORZELLAN-MANUFAKTUR NYMPHENBURGER

This famous porcelain manufacturer still turns out traditional rococo designs. Based in Nymphenburg Palace, with this outlet downtown.

🗺 N24 ✉ Odeonsplatz 1 ☎ 28 24 28 🕐 Mon–Fri 10–6:30; Sat 10–4 🚇 U-Bahn Odeonsplatz

RAHMEN-MAYR

You will always remember your visit to Munich if you take home a print, etching, or original painting of the city from here.

🗺 O24 ✉ Reichenbachstrasse 26 ☎ 201 45 63 🚇 U-Bahn Fraunhoferstrasse

SCHWABINGER TRÖDELMARKT

The city's most attractive collection of antiques and junk stores of all styles and genres. A great place to make for on a rainy day.

🗺 J25 ✉ Neusserstrasse 21 🕐 Fri and Sat only 🚇 U-Bahn Alte Heide

SPIELWAREN SCHMIDT

One of the big names in toys. Steiff bears and stuffed animals are this store's specialty.

🗺 N23 ✉ Neuhauser Strasse 31 ☎ 231 86 02 🚇 U- or S-Bahn Karlsplatz

STEIGERWALD

The city's top source for porcelain, silver, and glass.

🗺 N24 ✉ Amiraplatz 1 ☎ 22 42 00 🚇 U-Bahn Odeonsplatz

WORDS WORTH

Here, tucked away in a picturesque backyard, you will find a large range of English books, a charming Pooh Corner for children, and even a small British National Trust shop.

🗺 M24 ✉ Schellingstrasse 21a ☎ 280 91 41 🚌 53

Toys

Germany has been one of the world's leading toy manufacturers since the Middle Ages, and is particularly famous for its china dolls, tin plate toys, and Steiff teddy bears. Many important manufacturing centers are around Munich—Nuremberg, Oberammergau, and Berchtesgaden. Today, old Steiff bears are considered great collector's pieces; the record is for Teddy Girl, which was sold for $155,000 at auction in December 1994.

FASHION STORES

Chain stores

In recent years, traditional department stores have concentrated more on fashion and high technology in an attempt to win back the affluent shoppers who have switched their patronage to trendy boutiques and specialist retailers. The stores are offering more upmarket merchandise while weeding out everyday household goods and items that attract low profit margins.

BOGNER

This classic Munich company sells everything from sports clothes to traditional costumes for both men and women.

✚ N24 ✉ Residenzstrasse 15 ☎ 290 70 40 🚇 U- or S-Bahn Marienplatz

BREE

Stylish suitcases, handbags, wallets, belts, and more.

✚ N24 ✉ Theatinerhof, Salvatorstrasse 2 ☎ 29 87 45 🚇 U-Bahn Odeonsplatz

EDUARD MEIER

Munich's oldest shoe store, established in 1596, sells leather sofas. First-class service.

✚ N24 ✉ Residenzstrasse 22 ☎ 22 00 44 🚇 U- or S-Bahn Marienplatz

ESCADA

Escada was the first German designer label to make it big outside Germany and remains a classic, quintessentially German favorite.

✚ N24 ✉ Maximilianstrasse 27 ☎ 24 23 98 80 🚋 Tram 19

HALLHUBER

Leading labels at reasonable prices. Hallhuber is popular with young shoppers.

✚ L24 ✉ Leopoldstrasse 25 ☎ 38 30 81 10 🚇 U-Bahn Münchener Freiheit

HIRMER

A first-class clothing store with six floors exclusively for men.

✚ N23 ✉ Kaufingerstrasse 28 ☎ 23 68 30 🚇 U- or S-Bahn Marienplatz

KONEN

A reliable fashion store full of leading international labels.

✚ N23 ✉ Sendlingerstrasse 3 ☎ 23 50 20 🚇 U-Bahn Sendlinger Tor

PATAGONIA

The only Patagonia store in Germany sells stylish but practical sports clothing.

✚ L24 ✉ Leopoldstrasse 47 ☎ 39 92 99 🚇 U-Bahn Münchener Freiheit

RUDOLF MOSHAMMER

The sumptuous designs of flamboyant couturier Rudolf Moshammer draw princes and sheiks alike to his boutique on the Maximilianstrasse, now a Munich attraction.

✚ N24 ✉ Maximilianstrasse 14 ☎ 22 69 24 🚋 Tram 19

SCHLICHTING

A vast choice of fashion items for children, teens, and mothers-to-be, along with toys and games.

✚ N24 ✉ Weinstrasse 8 ☎ 29 16 45 35 🚇 U- or S-Bahn Marienplatz

STRUMPFHAUS LUDWIG BECK

Lovely lingerie, as well as stockings, and socks in every imaginable color.

✚ N24 ✉ Dienerstrasse 21, am Rathauseck ☎ 23 69 10 🚇 U- or S-Bahn Marienplatz

THERESA

Trendy and wildly expensive designer fashions, mainly Italian *prêt-à-porter*.

✚ N24 ✉ Maffeistrasse 3 ☎ 22 48 45 🚇 U-Bahn Odeonsplatz

MOVIE THEATERS & NIGHTCLUBS

MOVIE THEATERS

MOVIE THEATER
Probably the best movie theater in town, with four different movies daily, mostly undubbed.
✚ M22 ✉ Nymphenburger Strasse 31 ☎ 55 52 55 Ⓤ U-Bahn Stiglmaierplatz

IMAX
Germany's first IMAX movie theater shows fascinating nature films on giant screens.
✚ O24 ✉ Forum der Technik ☎ 21 12 51 80 Ⓢ S-Bahn Isartor

MUSEUM LICHTSPIELE
This former music-hall shows English-language movies.
✚ O24 ✉ Lilienstrasse 2 ☎ 48 24 03 Ⓢ S-Bahn Rosenheimerplatz 🚋 Tram 18

NEUES ARRI
One of Munich's main art movie theaters. Every November a competition for European Film Colleges is held here.
✚ M24 ✉ Türkenstrasse 91 ☎ 38 19 04 50 Ⓤ U-Bahn Universität

NIGHTCLUBS

KUNSTPARK OST
Huge on the all-night party scene, this hip cultural center has seven restaurants and eight clubs.
✚ P26 ✉ Grafingerstrasse ☎ 47 00 27 30 🕐 10:30PM–4AM Ⓤ U- or S-Bahn Ostbahnhof

NACHTWERK
This former warehouse offers plenty of space for dancing and is a popular venue for live bands.
✚ N20 ✉ Landsbergerstrasse 185 ☎ 578 38 00 🕐 10:30PM–4AM Ⓢ S-Bahn Donnersbergerbrücke 🚋 Tram 18, 19

P1
An extremely chic club in the basement of the Haus der Kunst with eight different bars frequented by models and celebrities.
✚ M24 ✉ Prinzregentenstrasse 1 ☎ 29 42 52 🕐 10PM–4AM Ⓤ U-Bahn Lehel

PARK CAFÉ
This huge club has long been a favorite, with music for all tastes in an unlikely rococo setting.
✚ N23 ✉ Sophienstrasse 7 ☎ 59 83 13 🕐 Tue–Thu 10PM–4AM Ⓤ U-Bahn Königsplatz

PFANNI FACTORY
In this old factory, Wolfgang Nöth, the Munich party mogul who specializes in large barnlike venues, continues the kind of event he first made his name for holding in the old Riem airport, now a trade fair center.
✚ P26 ✉ Grossinger Strasse 6 Ⓤ U- or S-Bahn Ostenhof

SKYLINE
New York-style bar and dance club, with breathtaking views over Leopoldstrasse.
✚ L24 ✉ Leopoldstrasse 82 ☎ 33 31 31 🕐 Mon–Thu 8PM–4AM; Fri–Sun until 5AM Ⓤ U-Bahn Münchener Freiheit

Movie theater events

It is hardly surprising that Munich is a city of movie-goers, with the Bavaria Film Studios, 84 movie theaters and a series of film festivals, including a Documentary Film Festival in April, the major *Münchner Filmfest* in Gasteig in June/July, a Fantasy Film Festival in July and International Art Film Week in August. The European Film Colleges Festival rounds off the year in November.

BARS, CAFÉS & LIVE MUSIC

All-night partying

Compared to that of other major European cities, Munich's nightlife is relatively small-scale and provincial; early closing laws prevent many places from staying open all night. Many bars close around 1AM and most nightclubs at 4AM. Still, if you know where to go, you can party till the wee hours. The Backstage Club, nicknamed "House of the Rising Sun," with its techno and house music doesn't even *open* until 6AM.

CAFÉ FRISCHHUT

Early birds meet night owls for coffee and delicious deep-fried *Schmalznudeln* pastries at 5 in the morning, here at the Viktualienmarkt.

🚋 N24 ✉ Prälat-Zistl-Strasse 8 ☎ 26 82 37 🕓 Mon–Sat 5AM–5PM 🚇 U- or S-Bahn Marienplatz

CAFÉ GLOCKENSPIEL

The roof-terrace cocktail bar, plush baroque-style bar and '70s-style Expresso bar-café at this place across from Marienplatz's famous Glockenspiel are always crowded.

🚋 N24 ✉ Marienplatz 28 (5th floor) ☎ 26 42 56 🕓 10AM–1AM 🚇 U- or S-Bahn Marienplatz

CAFÉ NEUHAUSEN

Mingle with a hip crowd at this stylish café with its long list of long drinks.

🚋 M21 ✉ Blutenbergstrasse 106 ☎ 123 62 88 🕓 Daily 10AM–1AM 🚇 U-Bahn Rotkreuzplatz

HAUS DER 111 BIERE

The name, House of 111 Beers, speaks for itself.

🚋 L24 ✉ Franzstrasse 3 ☎ 33 12 48 🕓 Mon–Thu 5PM–midnight; Fri and Sat 5PM–3AM 🚇 U-Bahn Münchener Freiheit

HAVANNA CLUB

Ernest Hemingway used to drink in this intimate bar decorated in Spanish colonial style.

🚋 N24 ✉ Herrnstrasse 30 ☎ 29 18 84 🕓 Mon–Wed 6–1; Thu–Sat 6–2; Sun 7–1 🚇 S-Bahn Isartor

INTERVIEW

A stylish crowd frequents this modern American bar from early morning till late at night.

🚋 024 ✉ Gärtnerplatz 1 ☎ 202 16 49 🕓 10–1:30AM; Sun until 7AM 🚌 52, 56

IRISH FOLK PUB

One of many popular Irish bars. This one pours 90 different malt whiskies, and serves up wholesome Irish food with live music on Thursdays.

🚋 L24 ✉ Giselastrasse 11 ☎ 34 24 46 🕓 8PM–1AM 🚇 U-Bahn Giselastrasse

JAZZCLUB UNTERFAHRT

One of Europe's most important jazz clubs with appearances from a roster of modern jazz, bebop, and avant-garde names.

🚋 026 ✉ Kirchenstrasse 96 ☎ 448 27 94 🕓 Tue–Sun 8PM–1AM; Fri and Sat until 3AM 🚇 S-Bahn Ostbahnhof 🚋 Tram 19

JODLER WIRT

This folksy, tiny, bar is straight out of the Bavarian countryside— always crowded and jolly, often with local yodellers at night.

🚋 N24 ✉ Alterhofstrasse 4 ☎ 22 12 49 🕓 Mon–Sat 7PM–3AM 🚇 U- or S-Bahn Marienplatz

JULEPS NEW YORK BAR

Spend a happy three hours here (5–8PM) with over 150 cocktails.

🚋 025 ✉ Breisacherstrasse 18 ☎ 448 00 44 🕓 Daily 7PM–1AM 🚇 S-Bahn Ostbahnhof

KAFFEE GIESING

Excellent live music, particularly jazz, blues, and rock, and classical music for breakfast.

⚓ Q23 ✉ Bergstrasse 5
☎ 692 05 79 🕐 Mon–Fri
4PM–1AM; Sat 11AM–1AM;
Sun 11AM–3PM 🚇 U-Bahn
Silberhornstrasse

MASTER'S HOME

An extraordinary underground bar in the colonial style of a typical African farmhouse. You can sit in the bathroom, the bedroom, the living room or at the bar, which is cooled by a giant airplane propeller, and eat, dance, or lap up the atmosphere over a delicious cocktail.

⚓ N24 ✉ Frauenstrasse 11
☎ 22 99 09 🕐 7PM–1AM;
weekends until 3AM
🚇 S-Bahn Isartor

MISTER B'S

A small atmospheric jazz bar with daily live concerts starting at 10PM.

⚓ 022 ✉ Herzog-Heinrich-Strasse 38 ☎ 53 49 01
🕐 Tue–Sun 8PM–3AM 🚇 U-Bahn Goetheplatz

NACHT CAFÉ

This 1950s-style bar is one of Munich's most popular places for live music ranging from jazz and blues to flamenco.

⚓ N23 ✉ Maximiliansplatz 5
☎ 59 59 00 🕐 9PM–6AM
🚇 U- or S-Bahn Karlsplatz

OKLAHOMA

Authentic saloon with live music.

⚓ R22 ✉ Schäftlarnstrasse 156 ☎ 723 43 27
🕐 Wed–Sat 7–1AM
🚇 U-Bahn Thalkirchen

SCHUMANN'S

It's often hard to get a table here, Germany's number-one bar, but once inside you can enjoy watching Munich's chic set, the *Schickeria*, at play. Tennis player Boris Becker is one of the regulars.

⚓ N24 ✉ Maximilianstrasse 36 ☎ 22 90 60 🕐 Mon–Fri
5PM–3AM; Sun 6PM–3AM
🚇 Tram 19

SCHWABINGER PODIUM

A small, popular venue that does rock'n roll and blues.

⚓ L24 ✉ Wagnerstrasse 1
☎ 39 94 82 🕐 Mon–Fri
8PM–1AM; Sat–Sun 8PM–3AM
🚇 U-Bahn Münchener Freiheit

WEINSTADL

The grand stone vaults of the oldest house in Munich provide a cozy venue for wine connoisseurs.

⚓ N24 ✉ Burgstrasse 5
☎ 28 58 90 🕐 Mon–Fri
11:30AM–3PM, 6:30PM–11PM
🚇 U- or S-Bahn Marienplatz

WINCHESTER ARMS

An English pub in the heart of Schwabing, complete with ale, darts, and pub food.

⚓ 023 ✉ Maistrasse 53
☎ 53 45 30 🕐 8PM–1AM
🚇 U-Bahn Goetheplatz

WUNDERBAR

This funky, cave-like bar is renowned for its fun crowd, futuristic décor, and late-night dancing.

⚓ N24 ✉ Hochbrückenstrasse 3 ☎ 22 88 00 75 🕐 8PM–4AM
🚇 U- or S-Bahn Marienplatz

Beer gardens

The Bavarian capital city's renowned beer gardens thrive from the first warm days of spring to the annual drinking climax of the Oktoberfest, when they are augmented by huge party tents erected on a downtown meadow (*Theresienwiese*). Before electrical refrigeration was invented, brewers had planted chestnut trees above their storage cellars to help keep supplies cool, then put out tables and benches in the shade to welcome drinkers. The 200-year-old Hirschgarten, the city's largest, has seating for 8,000 guests.

THEATER, CLASSICAL MUSIC, OPERA & BALLET

Musical mecca

Munich and music go hand-in-hand. The city's connection with Mozart, Wagner, and Richard Strauss, not to mention its three symphony orchestras, has made it famous throughout the world. Today it hosts a glamorous Opera Festival and the Summer Concert Season at Nymphenburg Palace. Try to attend one of the open-air concerts at the Residenz, held in an atmospheric courtyard in summer.

CUVILLIÉS-THEATER

Both opera and drama are popular at this magnificent theater, venue for the première of Mozart's *Idomeneo*, and considered the finest rococo theater in the world.

🚊 N24 ✉ Residenzstrasse 1 ☎ 2185-1940 Ⓤ U-Bahn Odeonsplatz

DAS SCHLOSS

Great theater classics are performed all year round in a giant tent on the outskirts of the Olympiapark.

🚊 K22 ✉ Ackermannstrasse 77 ☎ 300 30 13 🚋 Tram 27

DEUTSCHES THEATER

The number-one venue for musicals, revues, and ballet.

🚊 N23 ✉ Schwanthalerstrasse 13 ☎ 552 34 444 Ⓤ U- or S-Bahn Karlsplatz

GASTEIG

Home of the Munich Philharmonic Orchestra and the city's main cultural center (see panel opposite).

🚊 025 ✉ Rosenheimerstrasse 5 ☎ 48 09 80 Ⓢ S-Bahn Rosenheimer Platz

HERKULESSAAL

Munich's most impressive concert hall is in the Residenz.

🚊 N24 ✉ Residenzstrasse 1 ☎ 29 06 71 Ⓤ U-Bahn Odeonsplatz

HOCHSCHULE FÜR MUSIK

Young up-and-coming musicians from the Music Academy give regular free evening concerts and lunchtime recitals.

🚊 M23 ✉ Arcisstrasse 12 ☎ 28 92 74 41 Ⓤ U-Bahn Königsplatz

KOMÖDIE IM BAYERISCHEN HOF

Sophisticated light comedy is the specialty.

🚊 N23 ✉ Promenadeplatz 6 ☎ 29 28 10 Ⓤ U- or S-Bahn Karlsplatz

LACH UND SCHIESS-GESELLSCHAFT

Germany's most satirical revues are performed here.

🚊 L25 ✉ Haimhauser-Ursulastrasse Ecke ☎ 39 19 97 Ⓤ U-Bahn Münchener Freiheit

MÜNCHNER KAMMERSPIELE

The Munich Playhouse is one of Germany's best theaters. Tickets are like gold dust.

🚊 N24 ✉ Maximilianstrasse 26 ☎ 233 37000 Ⓤ U- or S-Bahn Marienplatz

MÜNCHNER MARIONETTEN-THEATER

A delightful puppet theater with shows especially for children in the afternoons and marionette opera performances for adults in the evenings.

🚊 023 ✉ Blumenstrasse 32 ☎ 26 57 12 Ⓤ U-Bahn Sendlinger Tor

MÜNCHNER THEATER FÜR KINDER

The German language proves no barrier for children in this magical theater where fairy-tales come alive. Favorites include

Pinocchio and Hänsel and Gretel.

🚇 M22 ✉ Dachauerstrasse 46 ☎ 59 54 54 🚇 U-Bahn Stiglmaierplatz

NATIONALTHEATER (BAVARIAN STATE OPERA)

The Nationaltheater is one of Europe's most respected operahouses. The excellent opera festival in July is the high point of Munich's cultural year.

🚇 N24 ✉ Max-Joseph-Platz ☎ 2185-1920 🚇 U- or S-Bahn Marienplatz

PRINZREGENTEN-THEATER

This theater was originally built to emulate the famous Wagner Festspielhaus in Bayreuth in 1900. Today, it stages plays, concerts, and musicals.

🚇 N25 ✉ Prinzregentenplatz 12 ☎ 21 85 29 59 🚇 U-Bahn Prinzregenten-platz

RESIDENZTHEATER

A modern theater with a broad repertoire of classical and contemporary plays.

🚇 N24 ✉ Max-Joseph-Platz 1 ☎ 21 85 19 40 🚇 U-Bahn Odeonsplatz

SCHLOSS BLUTENBURG

Spend an evening at this popular chamber music venue located in an atmospheric 15th-century moated castle (➤ 57).

🚇 L16 ✉ Obermenzing ☎ 891 21 10 🚇 S-Bahn Obermenzing

STAATSTHEATER AM GÄRTNERPLATZ

This flourishing theater claims to be the only municipal light opera-house in the world, with a wide repertoire of operetta, light opera, musicals, and ballet.

🚇 024 ✉ Gärtnerplatz 3 ☎ 201 67 67 🚇 U-Bahn Fraunhoferstrasse

THEATER BEI HEPPEL & ETTLICH

A glass of beer welcomes you to this relaxed student bar-cum-theater.

🚇 L24 ✉ Kaiserstrasse 67 ☎ 34 93 59 🚇 Tram 12, 27

THEATER DER JUGEND

Shows here appeal to both small children (morning and afternoon performances) and teenagers (evening shows).

🚇 L24 ✉ Franz-Joseph-Strasse 47 ☎ 23 33 71 71 🚇 U-Bahn Giselastrasse or Josephsplatz

THEATER IM MARSTALL

Avant-garde theater and experimental performances by the State Opera and the Residenztheater company.

🚇 N24 ✉ Marstallplatz 4 ☎ 21 85 19 40 🚇 U-Bahn Odeonsplatz

Gasteig

This modern complex, the city's main cultural center, lies at the center of Munich's music scene, focused on its splendid concert hall with its much-praised acoustics. There are concerts in the Carl-Orff-Saal, and during weekday lunchtimes students of the resident Richard Strauss Conservatory give free recitals in the Kleine Konzertsaal. Gasteig also houses Germany's largest city library and is the venue for the annual Film Festival, along with a full program of dance, experimental theater, movies, and jazz.

SPORTS & ACTIVITIES

Outdoor Munich

The Englischer Garten (English Garden) is a popular place for Munich's city dwellers to walk, cycle, or sunbathe. This extensive green space stretches from downtown along the banks of the River Isar. The Olympiapark, the stadium site of the 1972 Olympic Games, has been converted into a much-loved and much-used park with facilities including swimming, tennis, and ice-skating.

PARTICIPANT SPORTS

AMTLICHES BAYERISCHES REISEBÜRO

One of Bavaria's most enjoyable boating experiences. On a *Gaudiflossenfahrt*, a pleasure raft trip on the River Isar from Wolfratshausen to Thalkirchen, you will drift downstream to the music of a brass band and a steady flow of beer from the barrels on board.

✠ N22 ✉ Bahnhofplatz 2 ☎ 12 04 1 🚇 U- or S-Bahn Hauptbahnhof

BLUE UP

Don't let the name put you off this trip of a lifetime in a hot-air balloon, guaranteeing superb views of the Alps.

✠ L23 ✉ Lindenmannstrasse 2, Tutzing ☎ (08158) 13 60 🚇 S-Bahn Tutzing

BUNGEE JUMPING JOCHEN SCHWEIZER

Get a new perspective on Munich, hanging upside-down from a bridge.

✠ Off map to southeast ✉ Inselkammerstrasse2 ☎ 606 08 90 🚇 S-Bahn Taufkirchen

DANTEBAD

Swim while it snows at this outdoor pool—open all year.

✠ K21 ✉ Dantestrasse 17 ☎ 23 61 79 84 🚌 83, 177

DEUTSCHER ALPENVEREIN

This Alpine walkers' club organizes walking excursions in the mountains. Why not tackle the nearby Zugspitze, Germany's highest mountain?

✠ N24 ✉ Praterinsel 5 ☎ 14 00 30 🚊 Tram 17, 19

FELDAFING GOLF CLUB

One of the finest golf courses in Europe, overlooking Starnberger See.

✠ Off map to southwest ✉ Feldafing ☎ (08157) 93340 🚇 S-Bahn Feldafing

HEALTHLAND PRINZ

Pump iron with the likes of Boris Becker at Munich's trendiest health club.

✠ N26 ✉ Prinzregentenplatz 9 ☎ 41 20 02 00 🚇 U-Bahn Prinzregentenplatz

ISAR-BOWLING

One of Munich's biggest ten-pin bowling alleys, with special Moonlight-Disco-Bowling on weekends.

✠ Q24 ✉ Martin-Luther-Strasse 22 ☎ 692 45 12 🚇 U-Bahn Silberhornstrasse

MAX SCHROPP

On the Starnberger See, a beautiful lake with an Alpine backdrop, you can learn to windsurf or rent a sailboat.

✠ Off map to south ✉ Seepromenade Boothaus 4, Starnberg ☎ (08151) 162 52 🚇 S-Bahn Starnberg

MÜLLERSCHES VOLKSBAD

Germany's best swimming pool, in the *Jugendstil* style. Indoors.

✠ O24 ✉ Rosenheimer Strasse 1 ☎ 23 61 34 34 🚌 Tram 18 🚇 S-Bahn Isartor

OLYMPIA-EISSTADION
Curling, a traditional Alpine sport, is held on Thursday evenings at the Olympic Ice Stadium. Exhilarating and fun.

➕ J22 **☎** 30 67 21 50
Ⓤ U-Bahn Olympiazentrum

OLYMPIC PARK SKATING RINK
Rent your ice skates when you arrive at the door and enjoy this magnificent rink.

➕ J22 **☎** 30 67 21 50
Ⓤ U- or S-Bahn Olympiazentrum

RADIUS TOURISTIK
You can rent a bike at the main train station and explore the city on its 800 miles of bike paths. The tourist office's *Discover Munich* brochure will help you plan your route.

➕ N22 **✉** Hauptbahnhof (near platform 31) **☎** 59 61 13
Ⓤ U- or S-Bahn Hauptbahnhof

REITVEREIN CORONA
Get out of the city and explore the Bavarian countryside on horseback.

➕ Off map to south
✉ Muttenthalerstrasse 31
☎ 79 80 80 **Ⓤ** S-Bahn Solln

SPORT-SCHECK
It takes an hour by car to the nearest ski slopes; this department store will organize your trip.

➕ N23 **✉** Sendlinger-strasse 85 **☎** 21 66 12 54
Ⓤ U-Bahn Sendlinger Tor

TENNISANLAGEN OLYMPIAPARK
Tennis buffs can enjoy a game here. It is essential to make reservations in advance.

➕ K21 **☎** 30 67 24 15
Ⓔ Tram 20, 21

SPECTATOR SPORTS

SOCCER
The atmosphere is electric when FC Bayern München or TSV 1860 play their home matches in the Olympic Stadium.

➕ K22 **☎** 6 99 310
Ⓤ U-Bahn Olympiazentrum

HORSE-BACK RACING
Flat horse-back racing is held weekly at the racetrack in Riem from March through November, while trotting races are held in nearby Daglfing (**☎** 930 00 10).

➕ Off map to east
✉ Graf-Lehndorff-Strasse 36
☎ 94 55 230 **Ⓤ** S-Bahn Riem

TENNIS
The annual Compaq Grand Slam five-day tennis tournament, held in December, has developed into one of the most prestigious and glamorous events in international tennis with one of the biggest sporting cash prizes in the world.

➕ J22 **✉** Olympiahalle
☎ 95 72 57 14 (ticket office)
Ⓤ U-Bahn Olympiazentrum

Soccer fever
It is hardly surprising that football is Bavaria's most popular sport. FC Bayern München and TSV 1860 München are at the top of the German league, and there is an international player in virtually every position respectively. When the teams are playing at home, massive crowds throng the terraces, decked from head to foot in red-and-white (Bayern) or blue-and white (TSV 1860), filling the Olympic Stadium to its capacity of 70,000.

Attractive landscapes
The nearby towering Bavarian Alps and lakes remain popular destinations for Munich inhabitants seeking fresh air and recreation. On summer weekends many people escape the city to enjoy boating on the placid lakes or exhilarating walks in the picturesque countryside. In winter, skiers take to the road for the hour's journey to the snow-laden mountains.

LUXURY HOTELS

Prices

Expect to pay the following per night for a double room:

Luxury – over DM300;
153 euros

Mid-Range – up to DM300;
153 euros

Budget – up to DM150;
76.5 euros

Hotel scene

Like any metropolis, Munich can proudly claim a clutch of first-class hotels of worldwide reputation, but most of the city's 350 establishments are in the medium to lower price ranges. Except, that is, when a trade fair or the Oktoberfest beer festival takes place, when prices can increase substantially. The Upper Bavarian countryside south of Munich is well geared to welcoming tourists, thus offering the choice of staying in a nearby smaller town and commuting to the city by S-Bahn, train, or bus.

BAYERISCHER HOF

A classic, family-run Munich hotel with 398 rooms. Its excellent facilities include a roof-garden health club, swimming pool, and several good restaurants.
✚ N23 ✉ Promenadeplatz 2–6 ☎ 212 00 🚇 U- or S-Bahn Marienplatz

EXCELSIOR

In the tranquil pedestrian zone, three minutes' walk from the main station. 113 rooms.
✚ N23 ✉ Schützenstrasse 11 ☎ 55 13 70 🚇 U- or S-Bahn Hauptbahnhof

HILTON PARK

The Hilton has 479 rooms plus outdoor dining, beer garden, indoor pool, business center, and views over the English Garden.
✚ M25 ✉ Am Tucherpark 7 ☎ 38 45 0 🚇 U-Bahn Giselastrasse 🚌 54

DER KÖNIGSHOF

One of Munich's top hotels, with 90 rooms and one of the city's best restaurants.
✚ N23 ✉ Karlsplatz 25 ☎ 55 13 60 🚇 U- or S-Bahn Karlsplatz

OPERA

This small, homey hotel, with only 50 beds, is set in a delightful old mansion with an attractive inner courtyard.
✚ N24 ✉ St-Anna-Strasse 10 ☎ 22 55 33 🚇 U-Bahn Lehel

PLATZL

A friendly hotel with 170 traditionally decorated rooms. Top-class facilities include a health club and a beautiful restaurant in a converted mill.
✚ N24 ✉ Sparkassenstrasse 10 ☎ 23 70 30 🚇 U- or S-Bahn Marienplatz

PRINZREGENT

An elegant, rustic setting at this popular hotel, with 80 rooms and an attractive garden for breakfast and aperitifs.
✚ N25 ✉ Ismaningerstrasse 42-44 ☎ 41 60 50 🚇 U-Bahn Max-Weber-Platz

RAFFAEL

Royalty and celebrities have stayed at this 73-room, luxury hotel.
✚ N24 ✉ Neuturmstrasse 1 ☎ 29 09 80 🚇 U- or S-Bahn Marienplatz

RITZI

The aptly-named Ritzi is central yet quiet, with 25 stylish and beautifully decorated rooms. It has a trendy bar and serves a great buffet breakfast.
✚ M25 ✉ Maria-Theresiastrasse 2a ☎ 419 50 30 🚇 U-Bahn Münchener Freiheit

VIER JAHRESZEITEN KEMPINSKI

Munich's flagship hotel. Perfectly placed on Munich's most exclusive shopping street and within easy walking distance of most of the main sights, this was established as a guest house for royalty visiting King Maximilian II and is still used today to accommodate visiting dignitaries. 316 rooms.
✚ N24 ✉ Maximilianstrasse 17 ☎ 21 25 0 🚇 U-Bahn Odeonsplatz 🚋 Tram 19

MID-RANGE HOTELS

ADMIRAL
A smart Hotel Garni with 50 rooms, near the river and the Deutsches Museum. Special weekend packages.
➕ 024 ✉ Kohlstrasse 9 ☎ 21 63 50 🚇 S-Bahn Isartor

BIEDERSTEIN
A 45-bed hotel in a quiet Schwabing backstreet.
➕ L25 ✉ Keferstrasse 18 ☎ 38 99 970 🚇 U-Bahn Münchener Freiheit

CARLTON
A treasured secret for those in the know, this 59-room hotel is very reasonably priced for its location, a stone's throw from Odeonsplatz.
➕ M24 ✉ Fürstenstrasse 12 ☎ 28 20 61 🚇 U-Bahn Odeonsplatz.

COSMOPOLITAN
This simple, modern, hotel is surprisingly quiet considering its location in the heart of Schwabing. 71 rooms.
➕ L24 ✉ Hohenzollernstrasse 5 ☎ 38 38 1-0 🚇 U-Bahn Giselastrasse, Münchener Freiheit 🚊 33

EXQUISIT
A small, elegant hotel with a choice of 50 rooms, in a secluded side street near Karlsplatz, Marienplatz and the Oktoberfest site.
➕ N23 ✉ Pettenkoferstrasse 3 ☎ 551 99 00 🚇 U-Bahn Sendlinger Tor

GÄSTEHAUS ENGLISCHER GARTEN
Reserve well in advance if you want to stay at this oasis on the edge of the English Garden. There are only 12 rooms in the main building and 13 in the annexe.
➕ L25 ✉ Liebergesellstrasse 8 ☎ 38 39 410 🚇 U-Bahn Münchener Freiheit

INSELMÜHLE
This beautifully renovated, half-timbered corn mill is one of the Romantik chain of hotels and has 37 rooms. It is outside the center of the city but worth the extra trip.
➕ J17 ✉ Von-Kahr-Strasse 87 ☎ 810 10 🚇 S-Bahn Allach

PARK PLAZA
In the heart of the Schwabing area, this modern, 156-room hotel makes a convenient base for sightseeing and dining out.
➕ L24 ✉ Leopoldstrasse 132 ☎ 361 95 70 🚇 U-Bahn Münchener Freiheit

SPLENDID
A small, exclusive, downtown hotel, with only 35 rooms. Rooms are decorated in a range of styles including baroque, Louis XIV, and Bavarian.
➕ N24 ✉ Maximilianstrasse 54 ☎ 29 66 06 🚇 U-Bahn Lehel

TORBRÄU
An established, traditional hotel with 86 rooms, in the heart of Munich's Old Town. Facilities include an Italian restaurant, café, and *confiserie*.
➕ N24 ✉ Tal 41 ☎ 24 23 40 🚇 S-Bahn Isartor

Bookings
Wherever you see the following signs—*Hotel, Pension, Gasthof, Gasthaus, Gaststätte, Gästehaus, Fremdenzimmer,* and *Ferienwohnungen*—you will find accommodations. Make reservations as early as possible for the summer period and the Oktoberfest. Prices quoted always include service and taxes, and usually breakfast.

BUDGET ACCOMMODATIONS

Camping

For really inexpensive accommodations in Munich, why not bring a tent? There are three campsites in and around Munich. The best, and the most central, is Camping Thalkirchen (☎ 723 17 07), attractively positioned along the River Isar, with 700 places open from mid-March until the end of October. There is no need to book except during the Oktoberfest.

AM MARKT
A traditional hotel with 32 rooms, on one of the remaining original old squares near the Viktualienmarkt.
✚ N24 ✉ Heiliggeiststrasse 6 ☎ 22 50 14 🚇 U- or S-Bahn Marienplatz

BED AND BREAKFAST
This company organizes rooms in private homes and apartments in the downtown area and outskirts.
✚ M21 ✉ Schulstrasse 36 ☎ 168 87 81 🚇 U-Bahn Rotkreuzplatz

BLAUER BOCK
A comfortable hotel offering 75 homey rooms with parking available in the downtown area. Great value.
✚ N23 ✉ Sebastiansplatz 9 ☎ 23 17 80 🚇 U- or S-Bahn Marienplatz

BURG SCHWANECK
A youth hostel in a castle overlooking the River Isar. It's a long way from downtown but it is well worth the S-Bahn journey to stay. A valid youth hostel pass is required in order to stay here.
✚ Off map to south ✉ Burgweg 4–6, Pullach ☎ 793 06 43 🚇 S-Bahn Pullach

HAUS INTERNATIONAL
Slightly more expensive than youth hostels but you don't have to belong to a youth hostel organization to stay here.
✚ L23 ✉ Elisabethstrasse 87 ☎ 12 00 60 🚇 U-Bahn Hohenzollernplatz

JUGENDHERBERGE MÜNCHEN (MUNICH YOUTH HOSTEL)
Advance reservations and a youth hostel pass are essential here.
✚ M21 ✉ Wendl-Dietrich-Strasse 20 ☎ 13 11 56 🚇 U-Bahn Rotkreuzplatz

MITWOHNBÖRSE– HOME COMPANY
Useful for longer stays in Munich, the Mitwohnzentrale will arrange apartment accommodations for a small fee.
✚ L23 ✉ Georgenstrasse 45 ☎ 19445 🚇 U-Bahn Josephsplatz

PENSION FRANK
Models in town for photo calls often stay in this popular hotel, with 18 reasonably priced rooms, in the heart of trendy Schwabing.
✚ M24 ✉ Schellingstrasse 24 ☎ 28 14 51 🚇 U-Bahn Universität

SCHILLERHOF
This inexpensive, simple, well-run pension is located near the main train station and has 22 rooms.
✚ N23 ✉ Schillerstrasse 21 ☎ 59 42 70 🚇 U- or S-Bahn Hauptbahnhof

STEFANIE
A clean, friendly pension in the popular university district, a short distance from the Neue and the Alte Pinakothek. The accommodations comprise 32 rooms.
✚ M24 ✉ Türkenstrasse 35 ☎ 28 81 40 🚇 U-Bahn Universität

MUNICH
travel facts

ARRIVING & DEPARTING

Before you go

- EU nationals need a valid passport or a national identity card. Citizens of the U.S., Canada, Australia, and New Zealand need a valid passport to stay for up to three months. Other nationals should check visa requirements with the German Embassy.

When to go

- June to August are the warmest months; May to July tends to be the wettest time of year; and December to February are the coldest months.

Climate

- Average temperatures:
  January 34°F;
  April 57°F;
  July 76°F;
  October 57°F.

Arriving by air

- Munich's international airport, Flughafen München Franz-Josef-Strauss, is 19 miles from downtown.
- ☎ 97 52 13 13 for flight information
- Taxis from the airport are expensive.
- S-Bahn 8 and S-Bahn 1 run every 20 minutes (24 hours a day) to downtown.
  Bus routes take about 40 minutes to reach the main train station.
- An airport bus leaves Munich North Terminal every 20 minutes (5:50AM–8:55PM) taking 45 minutes to reach the main train station.

Arriving by train

- Trains take 18 hours to Munich from Calais or Ostend.
- Munich has good connections with most major European cities.
- Most trains terminate at the main station (Hauptbahnhof).
- The east station (Ostbahnhof) takes regular motorail services from other German stations and from Paris, Budapest, Athens, Istanbul, and Rimini.
- Train information from the German National Railway (Deutsche Bahn) is available in the main station's Travel Center (Reisezentrum) 🚩 N22 ☎ 233 302-57.

Arriving by car

- Munich is well served by highways, and a beltway provides easy access to downtown.
- Follow the clearly marked speed restrictions. Fines are harsh.
- Street parking is difficult in downtown. Use the parking lots.

Arriving by bus

- There are frequent bus links with other German cities, starting from the main bus terminal beside the main train station.

Customs regulations

- Duty-free limits for non-European Union visitors are: 200 cigarettes or 250g of tobacco or 50 cigars; 2 liters of wine and 1 liter of spirits.

ESSENTIAL FACTS

Electricity

- 220 volts; two-pin sockets. Take an adaptor with you.

Etiquette

- Say *Grüss Gott* (good day) and *Auf Wiedersehen* (goodbye) when shopping, *Guten Appetit* (enjoy your meal) when eating, *Entschuldigen Sie* (excuse me) in crowds.
- Never jump lights at pedestrian crossings. Do not walk on bicycle paths.

- Dress is generally informal, except for the theater, opera, or nightclubs.
- Although service charges are officially included in bills, tipping is customary and bills are rounded off to the nearest deutschmark.

Money matters

- On January 1, 1999, the euro became the official currency of Germany and the German deutschmark became a denomination of the euro. German mark bills and coins continue to be legal tender during a transitional period until July 2002. Euro bank bills and coins are likely to start to be introduced by January 1, 2002.
- All banks will change foreign bills during normal banking hours.
- Money-changing machines can be found at the airport, the main station and Marienplatz. Banks usually give better exchange rates.
- Munich has many exchange offices (*Geldwechsel*). The Reisebank exchange office in the main station opens from 6AM–11PM.

National holidays

- January 1, January 6, Good Friday, Easter Sunday, Easter Monday, May 1, Ascension Day, Pentecost and dau after Pentecost, Corpus Christi, August 15, October 3, November 1, 3rd/4th week in November: Day of Repentance and Prayer, Christmas Day, December 26.

Opening hours

- Banks: Mon–Fri 8:30–3:45 (some open Thu to 5:30, many close for lunch).
- Stores: Mon–Fri 9–6, may change to 9–8 (late shopping Thu until 8:30); Sat 9–2 , (but to 4 or 6PM on first Sat in the month). Many close for lunch (noon–2).

- Museums and galleries: Tue–Sun 9 or 10AM–5. Most close Mon and public holidays. Many free on Sun.

Places of worship

- Roman Catholic: Frauenkirche, Peterskirche, and many others.
- Roman Catholic Services in English: at 10:30AM in Kaulbachstrasse 33 and at 6PM in Kreuzkirche, Kreuzstrasse 2.
- Jewish: contact the Synagogue for details ✉ Reichenbachstrasse 27 ☎ 201 49 60
- Muslim: Mosque ✉ Wallnerstrasse 1–3 ☎ 32 50 61
- English services: International Baptist Church ✉ Holzstrasse 9; Evangelical International Community Church ✉ Enhuberstrasse 10

Student travelers

- Some museums and theaters offer up to 50 percent discounts with an International Student ID Card.
- A German Rail Youth Pass is available for young people under 26, valid for five, 10 or 15 days. Must be purchased outside Germany.
- For budget accommodations, camping and youth hostels (► 86).

Time differences

- It is 6 hours ahead of Eastern Standard Time in winter and 7 hours ahead in summer. Munich is one hour ahead of Greenwich Mean Time in winter and two hours ahead in summer.

Women travelers

- Frauenhaus München offers 24-hour help for women ☎ 35 48 30
- Some parking lots have well-lit, reserved parking for women only near the main entrance 🚹 025 ✉ Gasteig, Rosenheimerstrasse 5 🕐 8AM–midnight; 🚹 N23 ✉ Parkhaus am St-Jakobs-Platz, Oberangerasse 35–37 🕐 24 hours

Restrooms

- *Toiletten* are marked *Herren* (men) and *Damen* (women). *Besetzt* means occupied, *frei* means vacant. There is often a small charge.

PUBLIC TRANSPORTATION

- Munich has an excellent, albeit complicated, public transportation network, with two urban railways (S-Bahn rapid transit and U-Bahn subway), and a comprehensive network of bus and tram routes.
- The local transportation authority is the Münchner Verkehrs- und Tarifverbund (MVV) ✚ N24 ✉ Thierschstrasse 2 ☎ 41 42 43 44

Types of ticket

- The MVV network is divided into fare zones. Prices are based on the number of zones required to complete the trip. For most sightseeing you will remain in the *Innenraum* (interior area—marked blue on station maps). To travel farther you need a ticket valid for the *Gesamtnetz* (total network).
- Before boarding a train, you must put your ticket in the blue punching-machine (*Entwerter*) on the platform to validate it. On buses and trams you must immediately stamp your ticket upon boarding.
- Traveling without a valid ticket can result in a heavy fine.
- *Kurzstrecken*: short trip one-way tickets can be bought for journeys covering only four stops; two may be U- or S-Bahn stops. A trip must not last more than one hour and can only be used in one direction. Unlimited transfers are permitted.
- *Streifenkarte*: a strip of tickets. For each journey, stamp the appropriate number of strips. A "short trip" is one strip. More than two U- or S-Bahn stops within one zone is two strips. If you are traveling outside the blue *Innenraum* zone, a notice shows how many strips you need to punch.
- *Einzelfahrkarte*: one-way tickets can be bought covering any number of zones, but a *Streifenkarte* usually works out less expensive.
- *Tageskarte*: one day's unlimited travel from 9AM until 6AM the following day. Purchase either a *Single-Tages-Karte* for one person, or a *Partner-Tages-Karte* for up to five people (maximum two adults).
- *Stammkarte*: a personalized pass with a weekly ticket (*Wertmarke*). It's available from the MVV office at the main station. Bring your passport and passport photos.

Discounts

- People with disabilities who have a green/orange permit are entitled to travel free on MVV transportation.
- Children under four travel free.
- Children aged four to 14 travel at reduced fares.
- The Munich Welcome card, available from tourist offices, the main train station, and some hotels, provides unlimited travel for 24 hours on all public transportation plus savings of up to 50 percent on admission to major city attractions including museums, city tours, bicycle rentals, and the zoo. It is also available as a three-day ticket or a three-day partner ticket.

The U- and S-Bahn

- U-Bahn (subway) and S-Bahn (suburban trains) provide a regular service within 25 miles of the city center. Routes are referred to by their final stop.
- Underground trains run every 5 or 10 minutes from about 5AM–1AM.
- Tickets are available from automatic ticket machines at stations, MVV sales points in many stations, or in newspaper stores.

- Most U- and S-Bahn stations provide facilities for people with disabilities.
- Smoking is banned on trains and in the stations.
- Bicycles may be taken on the trains all day Saturday and Sunday and public holidays; on weekdays not at rush hour (6–8:30AM, 3–6:30PM).

Buses

- One-way tickets can be bought from the driver (with small change only). Multiple tickets, also valid for U- and S-Bahn, can be bought from vending machines at train stations, but not from the driver.
- Seven late-night bus lines and three tram lines operate between downtown and the suburbs once an hour from 1AM–4AM.

Trams

- Ticket procedures are the same as buses. Some trams have ticket-vending machines on board.
- Scenic routes: trams 18, 19, 20, 21, and 27 operate around the old town; tram 20 goes to the English Garden; tram 27 is useful for exploring Schwabing.
- Tram routes are numbered and the tram has a destination board showing where it is going to.

Maps and schedules

- MVV station ticket offices and tourist information centers supply free maps and information.

Taxis

- Taxis are cream-colored; stands are throughout the city.
- They are not particularly inexpensive; there's a small surcharge for luggage.
- Car rental: Hertz ☎ 550 22 56
- Central taxi stand ☎ 216 10
- Chauffeur service Sixt ☎ 21 03 10-00

MEDIA & COMMUNICATIONS

International newsagents

- Sussmann's Internationale Presse ✉ Hauptbahnhof ☎ 55 117 17 🕐 Daily 7AM–10:45PM

Newspapers and magazines

- Bavaria's daily paper, *Süddeutsche Zeitung*, is published in Munich.
- Munich has several local dailies—*Münchner Abendzeitung, tz*, and *Bild-Zeitung*, sold from newspaper boxes on street corners.
- There are no local English-language newspapers, but an English-language listings magazine, *Munich Found*, is available from major newsagent stores.

Post offices

- Main post office is across from the train station ✉ Bahnhofplatz 1 🕐 Mon–Fri 6AM–10PM, weekends and holidays 7AM–10PM
- Most other post offices are open Mon–Fri 8AM–noon, 3–6PM; Sat 8AM–noon.
- Mail boxes are bright yellow and clearly marked "Munich" and "other places" (*Andere Orte*).
- Cost for standard letter: European Union DM1,10 pfennigs; U.S.A., Australia and New Zealand DM3.
- Postcard costs: DM1,10 pfennigs; outside the European Union DM3.

Radio and television

- Münchners have access to around 20 TV channels, the main ones being ARD, ZDF, SAT 1, RTL, and Bayerisches Fernsehen.
- Satellite and cable channels include CNN (English-language sports channel), MTV, and SKY.
- BBC World Service Radio is available on 3955, 6195, 9410, and 1209 kHz. Also at night on 648AM.

91

Telephones

- Coin/phonecard telephones are cheaper than hotel telephones. Phonecards can be bought at post offices and newsagents.
- Make long-distance calls from boxes marked International or from telephones in post offices.
- Budget rate: between 6PM and 8AM on weekdays; all day on weekends.
- National enquiries 011 88.
- International enquiries 00 118.
- To call Munich from abroad, dial 00, followed by Germany's country code, 49 then the area code 89, followed by the number.
- To phone home from Munich, dial 00 followed by your own country code (UK 44, Ireland 353, USA and Canada 1, Australia 61, New Zealand 64), then the number.

EMERGENCIES

Embassies and consulates in Munich

- U.S.A. ⊠ Königinstrasse 5 ☎ 288 80
- U.K. ⊠ Bürkleinstrasse 10 ☎ 211 090
- Canada ⊠ Tal 29 ☎ 219 95 70

Emergency phone numbers

- Police ☎ 110
- Fire ☎ 112
- Ambulance ☎ 110 and 112 and 192 22
- Pharmacy emergency service ☎ 59 44 75
- Medical emergency service ☎ 192 22
- Dental emergency service ☎ 192 43
- Poisons emergency service ☎ 192 40
- Rape hotline ☎ 76 37 37
- Breakdown service ☎ 01802/5101112

Lost property

- Municipal lost property office: ⊠ Oetztalerstrasse 17 ⊕ Mon–Fri 8:30–noon Tue also 2–5:30 ☎ 233 45 901
- U-Bahn, trams, and buses: Fundamt ⊠ Arnulfstrasse 31 ⊕ Mon–Fri 8:30–noon ☎ 12 40 80
- S-Bahn: Fundstelle Im Ostbahnhof ⊠ Orleansplatz desk 8 ⊕ Mon–Thu 8–6, Fri 8–5 ☎ 13 08 4409
- For items left on Deutsche Bahn trains: Fundbüro der Bundesbahn ⊠ Hauptbahnhof, opposite platform 24 ⊕ Daily 6:30AM–11:30PM ☎ 13 08 66-64

Medical treatment

- EU visitors with a valid form E111 (obtainable from main post offices in your native country) can obtain free or reduced-cost emergency medical treatment.
- A list of English-speaking doctors is available at the British and U.S. Consulates.

Medicines and pharmacies

- Pack enough of any prescription medication you take regularly to last for the duration of your trip.
- Every neighborhood has a 24-hour pharmacy (*Apotheke*). Look for the address of that night's 24-hour *Apotheke* in the window.
- International pharmacies have staff who speak different languages. Try Bahnhof-Apotheke ✚ N22 ⊠ Bahnhofplatz 2 ☎ 59 41 19 or Internationale Ludwigs-Apotheke ✚ N23 ⊠ Neuhauserstrasse 11 ☎ 260 30 21 during store opening hours

Sensible precautions

- Munich is one of the safer European cities, but tourists should remain on their guard.
- At night, avoid poorly lit areas and the seedy red-light district behind the main train station.

Visitors with disabilities

- The MVV publishes a map with details of facilities for people with disabilities.
- Detailed information is available from the Munich Tourist Office.

TOURIST OFFICES

Tourist information offices

- Fremdenverkehrsamt München, ✉ Sendlingerstrasse 1 🕐 Mon–Thu 9:30–3, Fri 9:30–12:30 ☎ 233 0300
- Hauptbahnhof ☎ 233 30257 🕐 Mon–Sat 9–8, Sun 10–6
- Neues Rathaus ✉ Marienplatz 🕐 Mon–Fri 10–8, Sat 10–4

German National Tourist Offices

- U.S.A. ✉ 122 East 42nd Street, New York, NY 10168–0072 ☎ (212) 661 7200.
- U.K. ✉ PO Box 2695, London W1A 3TN ☎ 020 7317 0908

LANGUAGE

yes ja
no nein
please bitte
thank you danke
hello Grüss Gott
good morning guten Morgen
good evening guten Abend
good night gute Nacht
goodbye auf Wiedersehen ·
excuse me please entschuldigen Sie bitte
do you speak English? sprechen Sie Englisch?
I don't speak German ich spreche kein Deutsch
I don't understand ich verstehe nicht
today heute
yesterday gestern
tomorrow morgen
small klein
large gross
cold kalt
hot warm
good gut
menu die Speisekarte
breakfast das Frühstück
lunch das Mittagessen
dinner das Abendessen
white wine der Weisswein
red wine der Rotwein

beer das Bier
bread das Brot
milk die Milch
sugar der Zucker
water das Wasser
check die Rechnung
room das Zimmer
right/left rechts/links
straight ahead geradeaus
open/closed offen/geschlossen
near nahe
far weit
how much does it cost? wieviel kostet es?
expensive teuer
inexpensive billig
Where are the restrooms? Wo sind die Toiletten?
Where's the bank? Wo ist die Bank?
station der Bahnhof
airport der Flughafen
post office das Postamt
pharmacy die Apotheke
police die Polizei
hospital das Krankenhaus
doctor der Arzt

Monday Montag
Tuesday Dienstag
Wednesday Mittwoch
Thursday Donnerstag
Friday Freitag
Saturday Samstag
Sunday Sonntag

1 eins
2 zwei
3 drei
4 vier
5 fünf
6 sechs
7 sieben
8 acht
9 neun
10 zehn
11 elf
12 zwölf
20 zwanzig
50 fünfzig
100 hundert

93

INDEX

INDEX

Citypack
Munich

AUTHOR AND REVISION VERIFIER *Teresa Fisher*
COVER PICTURES *A. A. Photo Library*
INDEXER *Marie Lorimer*

Copyright   © Automobile Association Developments Limited 1997, 2001
Maps copyright © Automobile Association Developments Limited 1997, 2001
Fold-out map: © RV Reise- und Verkehrsverlag Munich · Stuttgart
                 © Cartography: GeoData

ISBN 0 6790 06893
First Edition

Acknowledgments
The Author wishes to thank Deutsche B.A., the Hotel Angleterre, the Munich Tourist Office, Michaela Netzer and Emmanuel Vermot for their help.
The Automobile Association wishes to thank the following photographers, libraries and museum for their assistance in the preparation of this book: Bridgeman Art Library, London 32b *The Laundress* by Edgar Degas; Mary Evans Picture Library 12; Teresa Fisher 8, 30, 39a; Edmund Nägele,FRPS 25a; Photo Press/Dr Brucker, 27a; Spectrum Colour Library 20; Toy Museum, Munich 23a, 60.
The remaining photographs are held in the Association's own library (AA Photo Library) and were taken by Clive Sawyer with the exception of pages 21, 53 which were taken by Adrian Baker and pages 7, 18, 23b, 24a, 25b, 26, 27b, 28a, 28b, 29a, 31a, 33b, 34, 35a, 35b, 38, 41a, 41b, 42a, 42b, 44, 47, 49b, 50a, 50b, 52, 55a, 56, 57, 61a, 87b taken by Tony Souter.

Important tip
Time inevitably brings changes, so always confirm prices, travel facts, and other perishable information when it matters. Although Fodor's cannot accept responsibility for errors, you can use this guide in the confidence that we have taken every care to ensure its accuracy.

Special sales
Fodor's Travel Publications are available at special discounts for bulk purchases (100 copies or more) for sales promotions or premiums. Special editions, including personalized covers, excerpts of existing guides, and corporate imprints, can be created in large quantities for special needs. For more information contact your local bookseller or write to Special Marketing, Fodor's Travel Publications, 280 Park Avenue, New York, NY 10017. Inquiries from Canada should be directed to your local Canadian bookseller or sent to Random House of Canada, Ltd., Marketing Department, 2775 Matheson Blvd. East, Mississauga, Ontario L4W 4P7.

Color separation by Daylight Colour Art Pte. Ltd., Singapore
Manufactured by Dai Nippon Printing Co. (Hong Kong) Ltd.
10 9 8 7 6 5 4 3 2 1

Titles in the Citypack series
- Amsterdam ● Barcelona ● Beijing ● Berlin ● Boston ● Brussels & Bruges ●
- ● Chicago ● Dublin ● Florence ● Hong Kong ● Lisbon ● London ●
- ● Los Angeles ● Madrid ● Melbourne ● Miami ● Montreal ● Munich ●
- ● New York ● Paris ● Prague ● Rome ● San Francisco ● Seattle ● Shanghai ●
- ● Singapore ● Sydney ● Tokyo ● Toronto ● Venice ● Vienna ● Washington, D.C. ●